Forty Gospel Greats for Banjo
by Eddie Collins

Intermediate Level

ISBN 978-1-57424-263-8
SAN 683-8022

Cover by James Creative Group

Copyright © 2010 CENTERSTREAM Publishing, LLC
P.O. Box 17878 - Anaheim Hills, CA 92817

www.centerstream-usa.com

All rights for publication and distribution are reserved.
No part of this book may be reproduced in any form or by any Electronic or mechanical means including information storage and retrieval systems
without permission in writing from the publisher, except by reviewers who may quote brief passages in review.

Table of Contents

Table of Contents

ABOUT THIS BOOK

This book is not an instruction method, rather a collection of old Gospel hymns. The book is primarily designed for intermediate level players. For purposes of this book, intermediate means the player attempting these songs is familiar with *Scruggs* style which uses right-hand *rolls* (a repetitive flow of notes) and *slurs* (hammer-ons, slides, pull-offs, and chokes). The intermediate player should also have a working knowledge of *Melodic* (Keith) style which maintains a flow of notes by continually varying the string each right-hand finger picks. *Single-String* (Reno) style utilizes left-hand scale patterns in a manner similar to a guitarist. Single-String style appears sparingly in this work.

The intermediate 5-string banjo player should be familiar with combining a left-hand melody with right-hand rolls. A working knowledge of chord formations, including moveable forms is helpful–especially when playing rhythm to the pieces.

TABLATURE AND TUNING

Tablature is a representation of the strings on the banjo. String number 1 is on top of the series of parallel lines. A number on the line represents the fret that is to be played on the given string. An "S" or "H" represents a <u>S</u>lide or <u>H</u>ammer-on. For more on tablature, see the guide on page 5. Standard G tuning (g DGBD – for strings 5 through 1) is used on all the songs. If a singer performs a song in a different key, you may wish to use a capo.

COUNTING BEATS

Most songs in this book are played in 4/4 (Common) time. Assume the piece is in 4/4 if no time signature is given This dictates you count four beats per measure with a series of 8th notes being counted 1 & 2 & 3 & 4 &. Several songs are played in 3/4 (waltz) time. Here, you count three beats per measure with a typical right-hand roll consisting of six eighth notes.

PLAYING WITH A BOUNCE

When listening to the CD, you will notice that some songs, especially those performed slowly, are played with an uneven feel called a *shuffle* or *bounce*. The music is written using 8th notes, but two 8th notes are played as a triplet with the first two notes tied. It is best to imitate the feel of the beat by replicating what you hear on the recording.

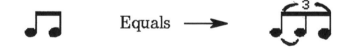

PERFORMANCE NOTES

Performance notes help you interpret each song and alert of potential tricky parts. Both parts of the song, verse and chorus, are given when the melody to each is distinctly different.

THE PRACTICE CD

The CD allows you to hear each solo at a comfortable learning speed. Tune to an electronic tuner and you will be in tune to the CD. The instruments are recorded with separation. Adjust your balance knob for more banjo to learn the piece, or more guitar to practice performing your solos. The track numbers are listed in the Table of Contents and on each individual solo.

TABLATURE GUIDE

Symbol	Name	Explanation
│	Measure Line	Separates notes into an equal number of beats
‖	Double Bar	Marks start or end of a section
‖:	Begin Repeat	Marks start of part played twice
:‖	End Repeat	Marks end of repeated section
1.	1st Ending	Play this ending 1st time through
2.	2nd Ending	Play this ending 2nd time through
3/4	Time Signature	Top # = # of beats per measure; Bottom # = the type of note that gets 1 count
♪	Eighth Note	Receives 1/2 count
│	Quarter Note	Receives 1 count
⊔	8ths Beam	Count 2 per beat
⊔	16ths Beam	Count 4 per beat
⊔³	Triplet	Count 3 per beat
₹	Quarter Rest	Rest 1 beat
♯	Eighth Rest	Rest 1/2 beat
▬	Half Rest	Rest 2 beats
·	Dot	Add 1/2 value of original note
⌢	Tie	Combines note values of two notes into one note
0	Zero	Play string open
2	Numeral	Number of fret to be played
c	Choke	Left hand bends note as right hand strikes string
s	Slide	Slide left-hand finger to sound second note
h	Hammer-On	Add second note without restriking the string
p	Pull-Off	Pull finger off to sound second note
⌇ b	Brush	Strum strings so as to hear each string

The Left-Hand Fingers
(palm up)

1 2 3 4

The Right-Hand Fingers
(palm up)

M I T

Angel Band

Traditional
Key of G

Arranged by Eddie Collins

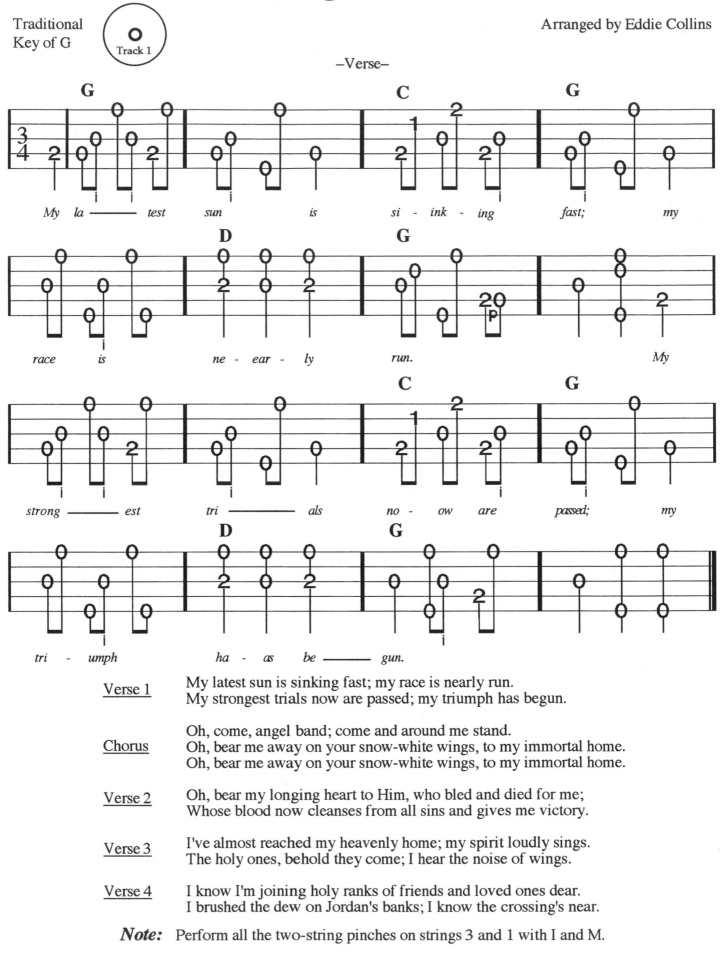

Verse 1 — My latest sun is sinking fast; my race is nearly run.
My strongest trials now are passed; my triumph has begun.

Chorus — Oh, come, angel band; come and around me stand.
Oh, bear me away on your snow-white wings, to my immortal home.
Oh, bear me away on your snow-white wings, to my immortal home.

Verse 2 — Oh, bear my longing heart to Him, who bled and died for me;
Whose blood now cleanses from all sins and gives me victory.

Verse 3 — I've almost reached my heavenly home; my spirit loudly sings.
The holy ones, behold they come; I hear the noise of wings.

Verse 4 — I know I'm joining holy ranks of friends and loved ones dear.
I brushed the dew on Jordan's banks; I know the crossing's near.

Note: Perform all the two-string pinches on strings 3 and 1 with I and M.

Angel Band

Traditional
Key of G

Arranged by Eddie Collins

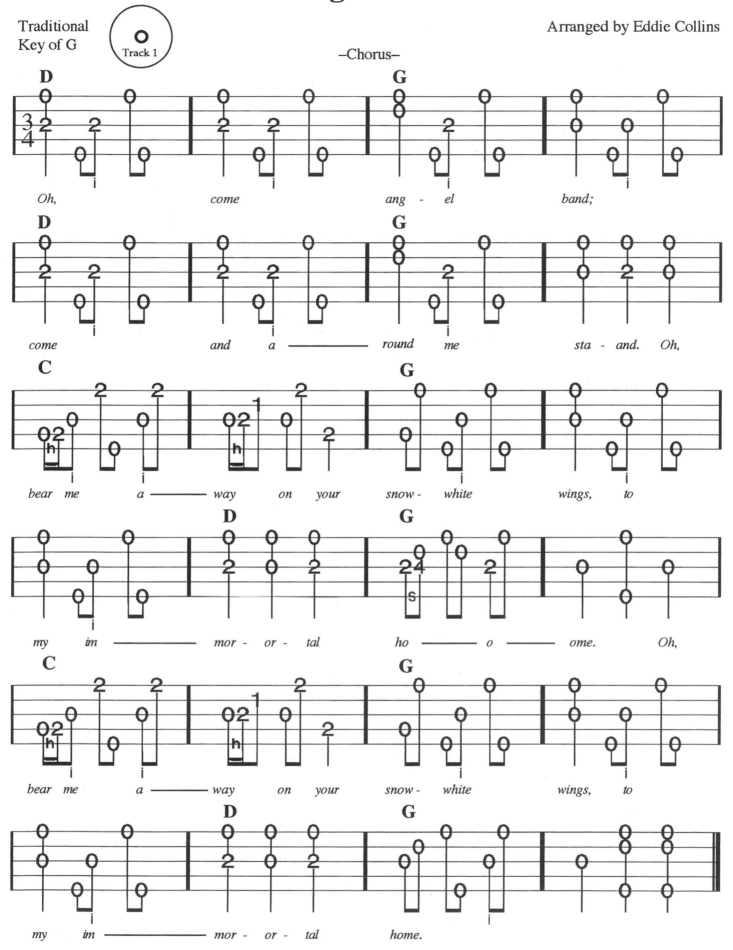

Are You Washed In The Blood?

Traditional
Key of G

Track 2

Arranged by Eddie Collins

–Verse–

Have you been to Jesus for the cleansing pow'r? Are you washed in the blood of the lamb? Are you fully trusting in His grace this hour? Are you washed in the blood of the lamb?

Verse 1

Have you been to Jesus for the cleansing power?
Are you washed in the blood of the Lamb?
Are you fully trusting in His grace this hour?
Are you washed in the blood of the Lamb?

Verse 2

Are you walking daily by the Savior's side?
Are you washed in the blood of the Lamb?
Do you rest each moment in the Crucified?
Are you washed in the blood of the Lamb?

Verse 3

When the Bridegroom cometh, will your robes be white?
Are you washed in the blood of the Lamb?
Will your soul be ready for the mansions bright?
And be washed in the blood of the Lamb?

Are You Washed In The Blood?

Traditional
Key of G

Track 2

Arranged by Eddie Collins

–Chorus–

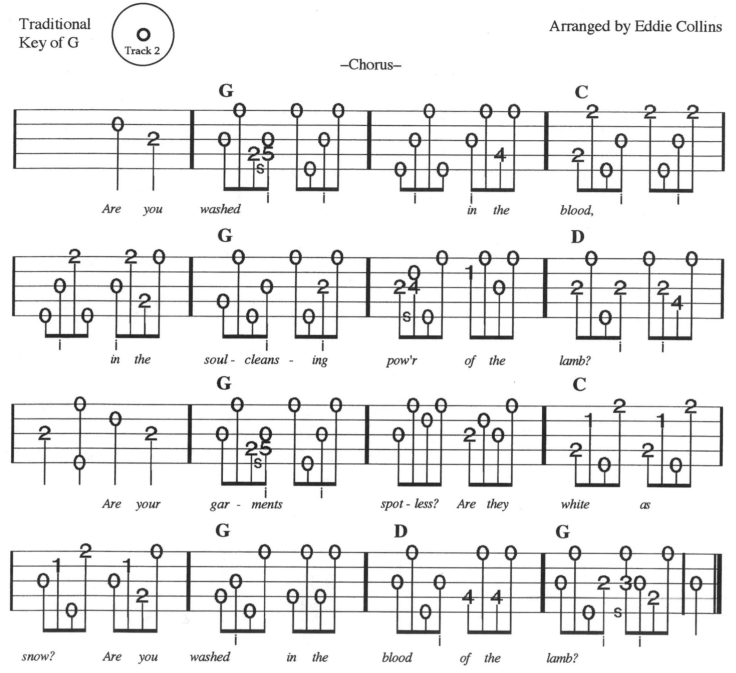

Chorus

Are you washed in the blood,
In the soul-cleansing blood of the Lamb?
Are your garments spotless? Are they white as snow?
Are you washed in the blood of the Lamb?

Verse 4

Lay aside the garments that are stained with sin,
And be washed in the blood of the Lamb.
There's a fountain flowing for the soul unclean,
O be washed in the blood of the Lamb!

Crying Holy Unto My Lord

Traditional
Key of G

Track 3

Arranged by Eddie Collins

–Chorus–

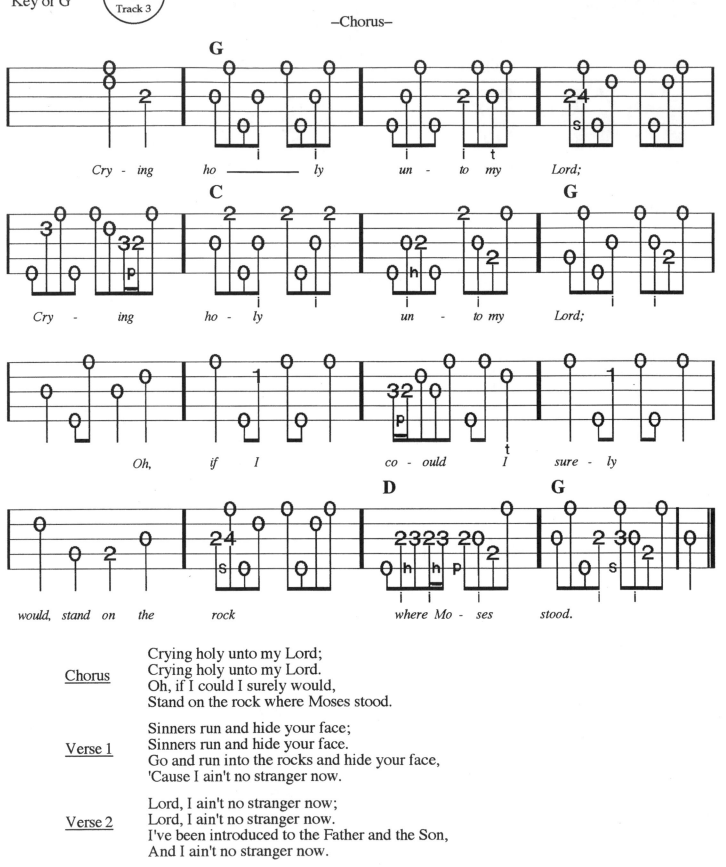

Chorus

Crying holy unto my Lord;
Crying holy unto my Lord.
Oh, if I could I surely would,
Stand on the rock where Moses stood.

Verse 1

Sinners run and hide your face;
Sinners run and hide your face.
Go and run into the rocks and hide your face,
'Cause I ain't no stranger now.

Verse 2

Lord, I ain't no stranger now;
Lord, I ain't no stranger now.
I've been introduced to the Father and the Son,
And I ain't no stranger now.

Note: All verses share the same melody as the chorus.

Do Lord, Remember Me

Traditional
Key of G

Track 5

Arranged by Eddie Collins

–Chorus–

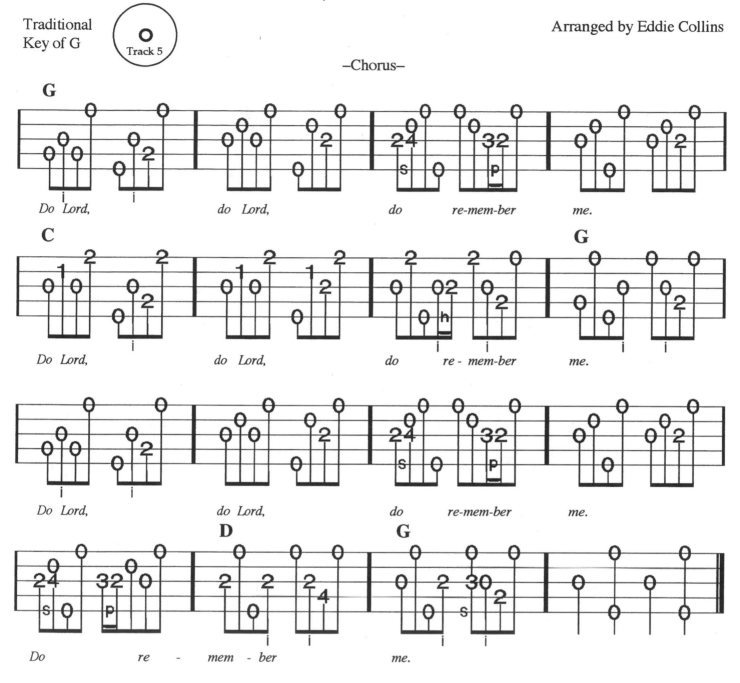

Do Lord, do Lord, do re-mem-ber me.

Do Lord, do Lord, do re - mem-ber me.

Do Lord, do Lord, do re-mem-ber me.

Do re - mem - ber me.

Chorus	Do Lord, do Lord, do remember me (3 times) Do Lord, remember me.
Verse 1	When I'm in trouble, do remember me (3 times) Do Lord, remember me.
Verse 2	When I am dying, do remember me (3 times) Do Lord, remember me.
Verse 3	When this world's on fire, do remember me (3 times) Do Lord, remember me.

Note: All verses share the same melody as the chorus. This is based on the old Negro Spiritual with the lyric being in the form of a command/request, not a question as in the more modern version, "Do Lord, Do You Remember Me?"

Day By Day

Traditional
Key of C

Track 7

Arranged by Eddie Collins

–Verse–

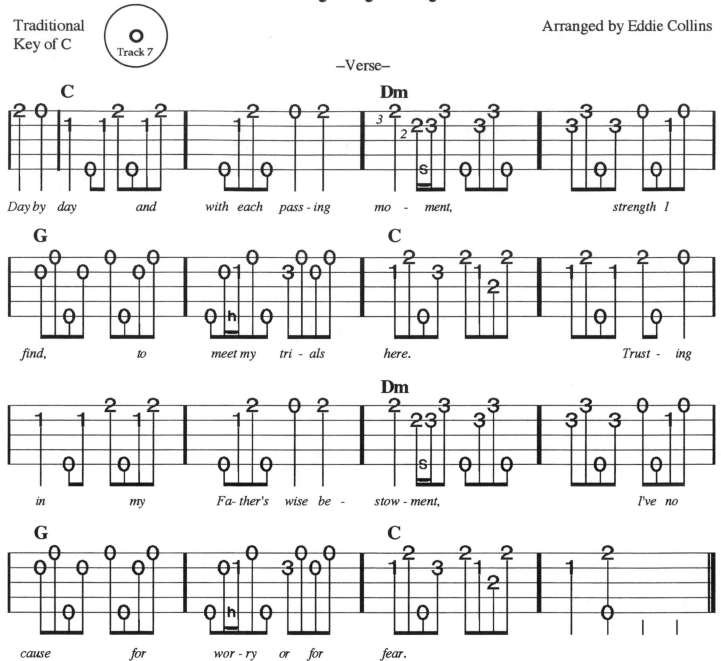

Verse 1

Day by day, and with each passing moment, strength I find, to meet my trials here.
Trusting in my father's wisdom bestowment, I've no cause for worry or for fear.
His whose heart is kind beyond all measure, gives unto each day what He deems best.
Lovingly, it's part of pain and pleasure, mingling toil with peace and rest.

Verse 2

Every day, the Lord Himself is near to me, with a special mercy for each hour.
All my cares He fain would bear and cheer me, He whose name is Counselor and Power.
The protection of His child and treasure, is a charge that on Himself He laid.
As thy days, thy strength shall be in measure, this the pledge to me He made.

Day By Day

Traditional
Key of C

Arranged by Eddie Collins

–Verse Continued–

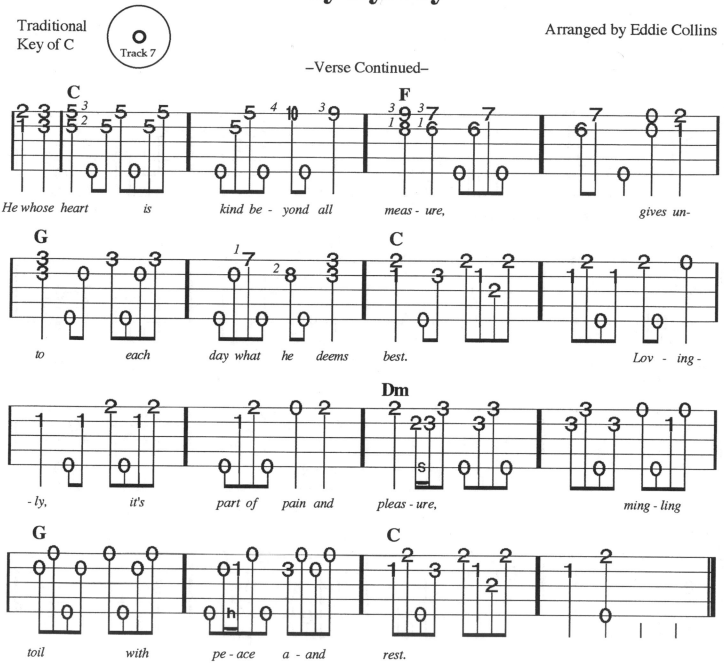

He whose heart   is   kind be - yond all   meas - ure,   gives un-

to   each   day what   he   deems   best.   Lov - ing-

- ly,   it's   part of   pain and   pleas - ure,   ming - ling

toil   with   pe - ace   a - and   rest.

Verse 3

Help me then in every tribulation, so to trust Thy promises, O Lord,
That I lose not faith's sweet consolation, offered me within Thy holy word.
Help me Lord, when toil and trouble meeting, E'er to take as from a father's hand,
One by one, the days, the moments fleeting, till I reach the promised land.

Down By The Riverside

Traditional
Key of G

Arranged by Eddie Collins

Track 8

–Verse–

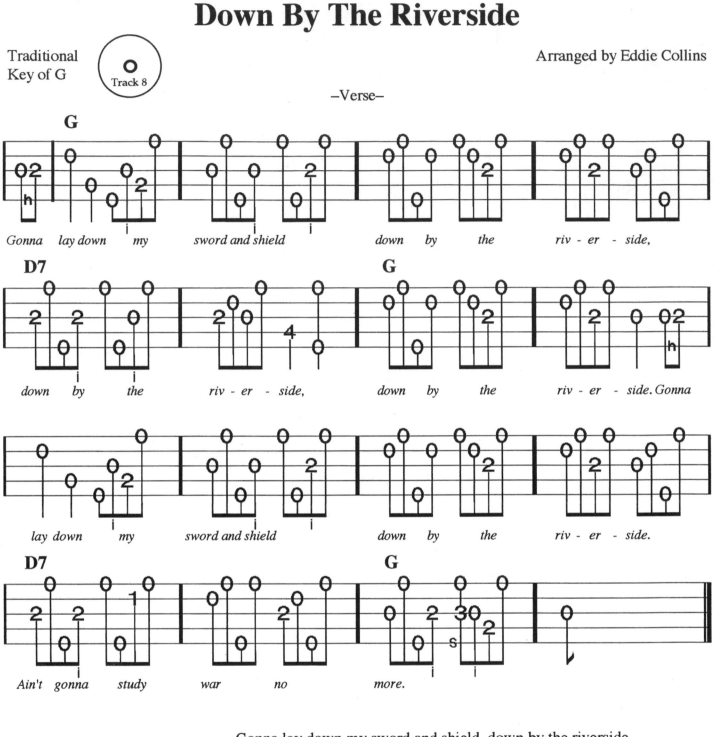

Gonna lay down my sword and shield down by the riv - er - side,

down by the riv - er - side, down by the riv - er - side. Gonna

lay down my sword and shield down by the riv - er - side.

Ain't gonna study war no more.

Verse 1
Gonna lay down my sword and shield, down by the riverside,
Down by the riverside, down by the riverside.
Gonna lay down my sword and shield, down by the riverside,
Ain't gonna study war no more.

Verse 2
Gonna lay down my burden, down by the riverside,
Down by the riverside, down by the riverside.
Gonna lay down my burden, down by the riverside,
Ain't gonna study war no more.

Verse 3
I'm gonna put on my long white robe, down by the riverside,
Down by the riverside, down by the riverside.
Gonna put on my long white robe, down by the riverside
Ain't gonna study war no more.

Down By The Riverside

Traditional
Key of G

Track 8

Arranged by Eddie Collins

–Chorus–

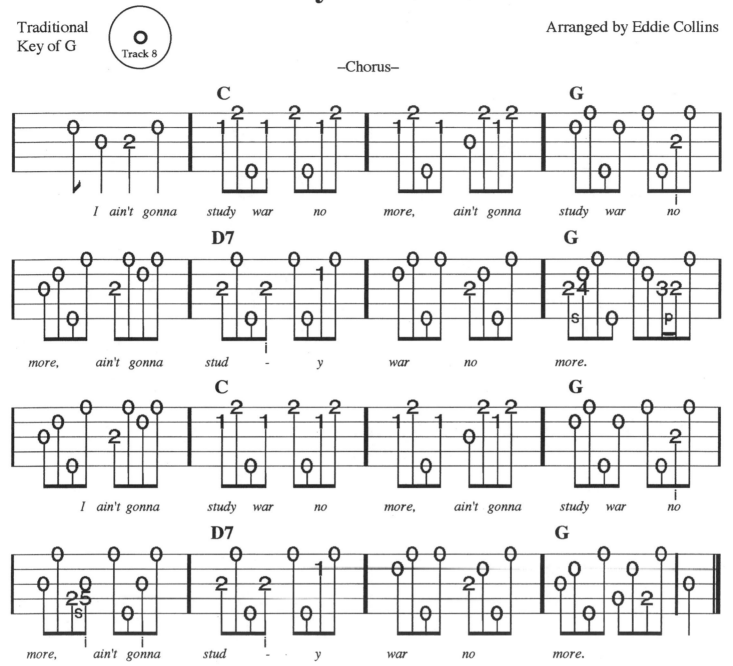

Chorus

I ain't gonna study war no more, ain't gonna study war no more,
Ain't gonna study war no more.

I ain't gonna study war no more, ain't gonna study war no more,
Ain't gonna study war no more.

Drifting Too Far From The Shore

Traditional
Key of G

Track 9

Arranged by Eddie Collins

–Verse–

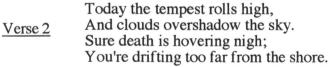

Out on the perilous deep, where dangers silently creep. And storms so violently sweep; you're drifting too far from the shore.

Verse 1
Out on the perilous deep,
Where dangers silently creep.
And storms so violently sweep;
You're drifting too far from the shore

Verse 2
Today the tempest rolls high,
And clouds overshadow the sky.
Sure death is hovering nigh;
You're drifting too far from the shore.

Note: Perform all the two-string pinches on strings 1, 2 and 3 with I and M.

Drifting Too Far From The Shore

Traditional
Key of G

Track 9

Arranged by Eddie Collins

–Chorus–

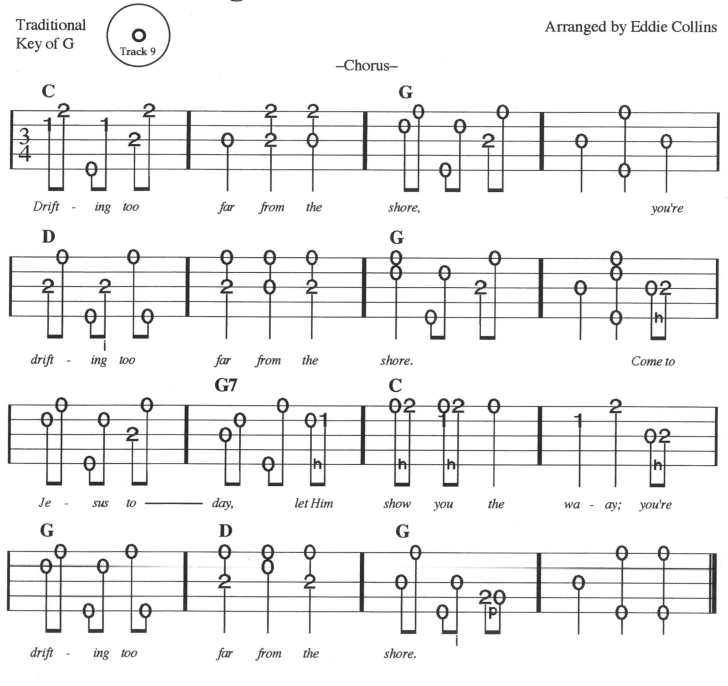

Drift - ing too far from the shore, you're drift - ing too far from the shore. Come to Je - sus to —— day, let Him show you the wa - ay; you're drift - ing too far from the shore.

Chorus

Drifting too far from the shore;
You're drifting too far from the shore.
Come to Jesus today, let him show you the way,
You're drifting too far from the shore.

Verse 3

Why meet a terrible fate,
Mercy abundantly waits.
Turn back before its to late;
You're drifting too far from the shore.

Note: Perform all the two-string pinches on strings 1, 2 and 3 with I and M.

Green Pastures

Traditional
Key of G

Track 10

Arranged by Eddie Collins

–Verse–

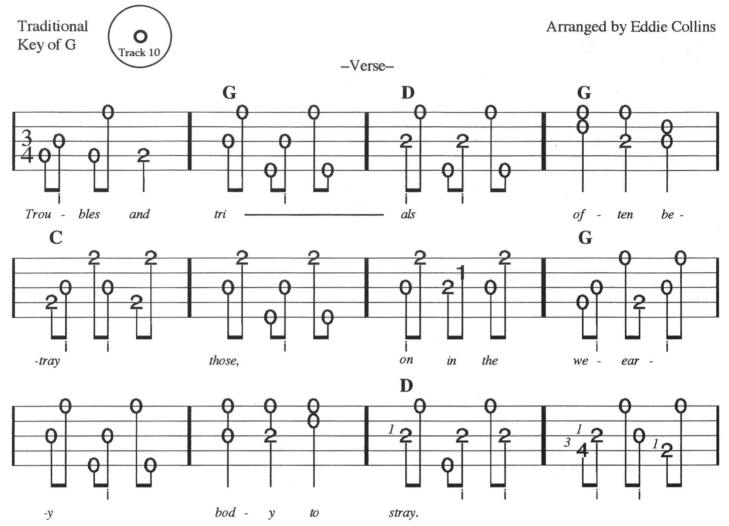

Trou - bles and tri ——————— als of - ten be -

-tray those, on in the we - ear -

-y bod - y to stray.

Verse 1
Troubles and trials often betray those,
On in the weary body to stray.
But we shall walk beside the still waters,
With the Good Shepherd leading the way.

Verse 2
Those who have strayed were sought by The Master,
He who once gave His life for the sheep.
Out on the mountain still He is searching,
Bringing them in forever to keep.

Verse 3
Going up home to live in green pastures,
Where we shall live and die never more,
Even the Lord will be in that number,
When we shall reach that heavenly shore.

Note: Perform all the two-string pinches with I and M. Hold the full chord during the C.

Green Pastures

Traditional
Key of G

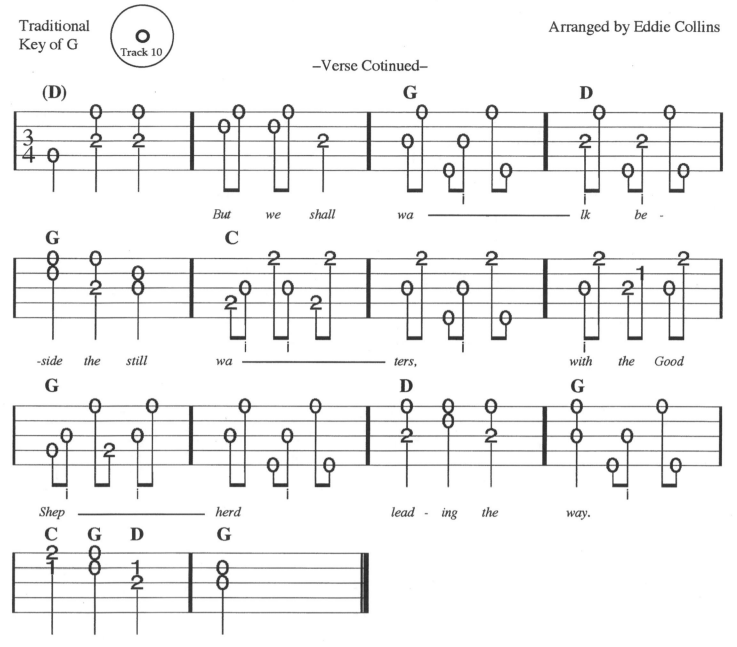

Track 10

Arranged by Eddie Collins

–Verse Cotinued–

But we shall wa ——————— lk be -

-side the still wa ——————— ters, with the Good

Shep ——————— herd lead - ing the way.

Verse 4
We will not heed the voice of the stranger,
For he would lead us to despair.
Following on with Jesus our savior,
We shall all reach that country so fair.

Verse 5
Going up home to live in green pastures,
Where we shall live and die never more.
Even the Lord will be in that number,
When we shall reach that heavenly shore.

Note: This song is a series of verses, each with the same melody.

Gospel Plow

Traditional
Key of G

Arranged by Eddie Collins

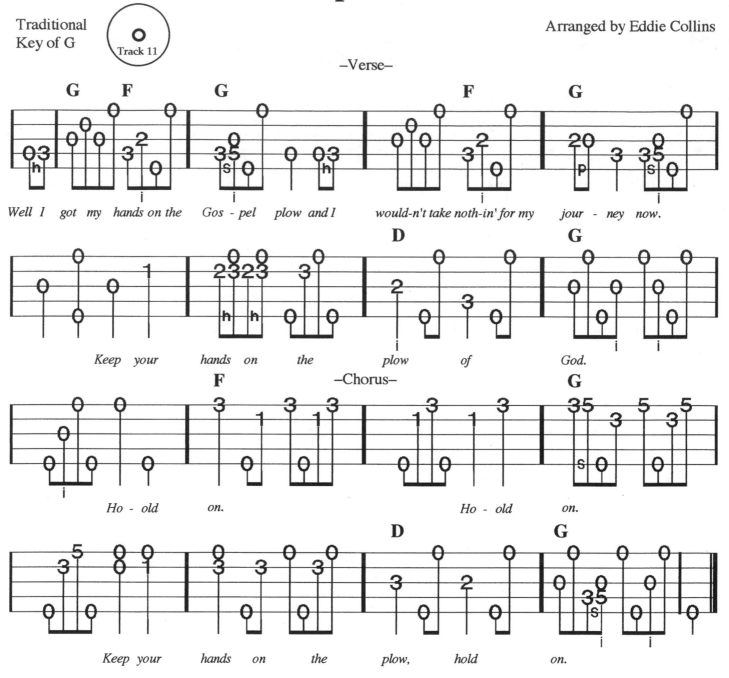

Verse 1   Well, I got my hands on the Gospel plow,
And I wouldn't take nothin' for my journey now. *

Chorus   Hold on. Hold on. Keep your hands on that plow, hold on.

Verse 2   Well, Matthew, Mark, Luke and John,
All those prophets are dead and gone. *

Verse 3   I never been to heaven, but I've been told,
The streets up there are made of gold. *

Verse 4   Sister Mary was bound in chains,
On every link was Jesus' name. *

*Insert the lyric "Keep your hands on the plow of God." as the last line of each verse.

He's Got The Whole World In His Hands

Traditional
Key of G

Arranged by Eddie Collins

–Verse–

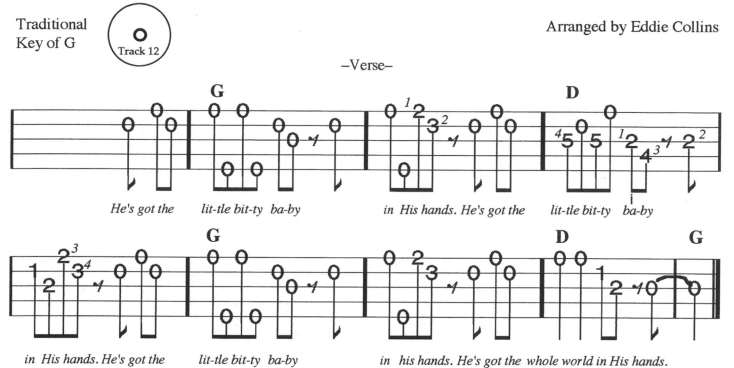

He's got the   *lit-tle bit-ty ba-by*   *in His hands. He's got the*   *lit-tle bit-ty ba-by*

in His hands. He's got the   *lit-tle bit-ty ba-by*   *in his hands. He's got the whole world in His hands.*

Chorus
: He's got the whole world in His hands.
He's got the whole wide world in His hands.
He's got the whole world in His hands.
He's got the whole world in His hands.

Verse 1
: He's got the little bitty baby, in His hands (3 times)
He's got the whole world in His hands.

Verse 2
: He's got you and me sister, in His hands (3 times)
He's got the whole world in His hands.

Verse 3
: He's got you and me brother, in His hands (3 times)
He's got the whole world in His hands.

In The Sweet By And By

Traditional
Key of G

Track 13

Arranged by Eddie Collins

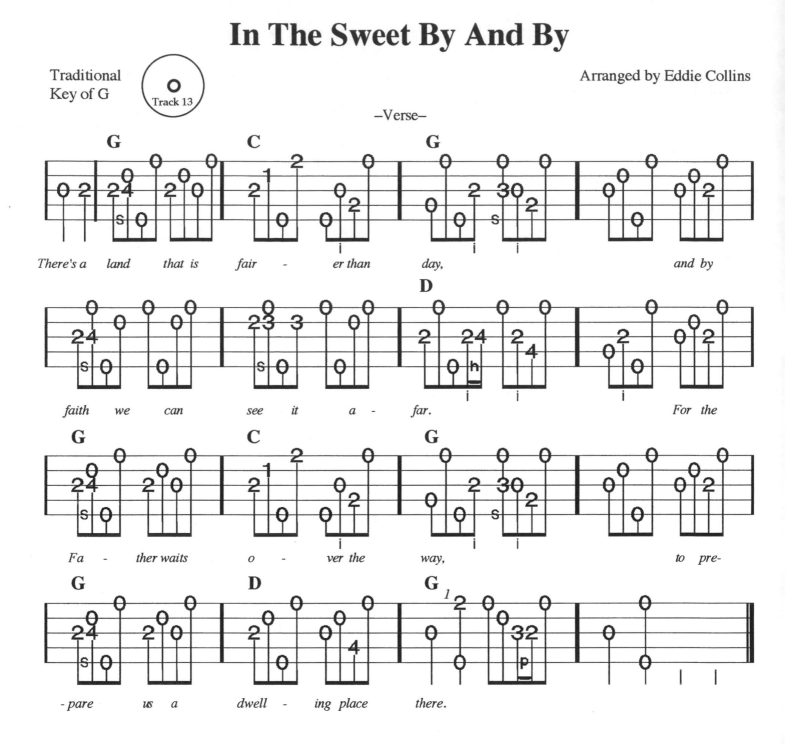

–Verse–

Verse 1 — There's a land that is fairer than day, / And by faith we can see it afar. / For the Father waits over the way, / To prepare us a dwelling place there.

Verse 2 — We shall sing on that beautiful shore, / The melodious songs of the blessed. / And our spirit shall sorrow no more, / Not a sign for the blessing of rest.

In The Sweet By And By

Traditional
Key of G

Track 13

Arranged by Eddie Collins

–Chorus–

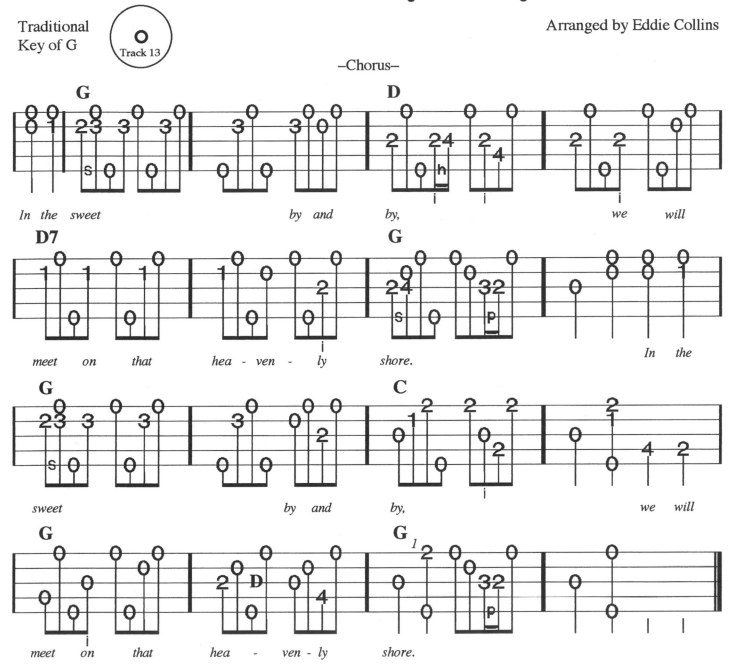

In the sweet ... by and by, ... we will

meet on that hea - ven - ly shore. ... In the

sweet ... by and by, ... we will

meet on that hea - ven - ly shore.

Chorus

In the sweet by and by,
We shall meet on that beautiful shore.
In the sweet by and by,
We shall meet on that beautiful shore.

Verse 3

To our bountiful Father above,
We will offer our tribute of praise.
For the glorious gift of His love,
And the blessings that hallow our days.

I Am A Pilgrim

Traditional
Key of G

Track 14

Arranged by Eddie Collins

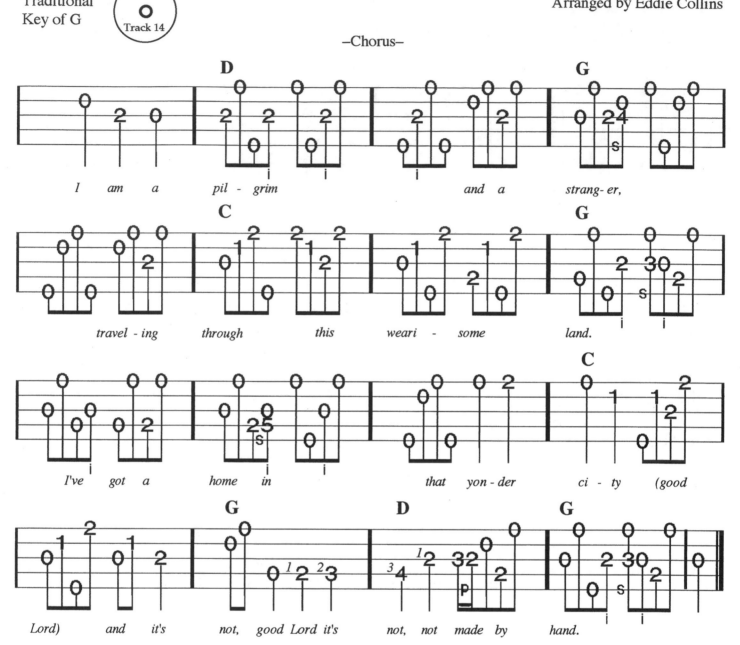

–Chorus–

I am a pil - grim and a strang- er, travel - ing through this weari - some land. I've got a home in that yon - der ci - ty (good Lord) and it's not, good Lord it's not, not made by hand.

Chorus	I am a pilgrim and a stranger, traveling through this wearisome land. I've got a home in that yonder city, good Lord, And it's not (good Lord it's not), not made by hand.
Verse 1	I got a mother, a sister and a brother who have gone this way before, I am determined to go and see them, good Lord, For they're on (oh Lord they're on) that distant shore.
Verse 2	I'm going down to the river of Jordan, just to soothe my weary soul, If I could touch but just the hem of His garment, good Lord, I believe (good Lord I believe), it would make me whole.
Verse 3	Now when I'm dead, laying in my coffin and my friends all gather round. They can say that he's just laying there sleeping, good Lord, Sweet peace (Lord sweet peace) his soul has found.

Jacob's Ladder

Traditional
Key of D
Track 15

Arranged by Eddie Collins

–Chorus–

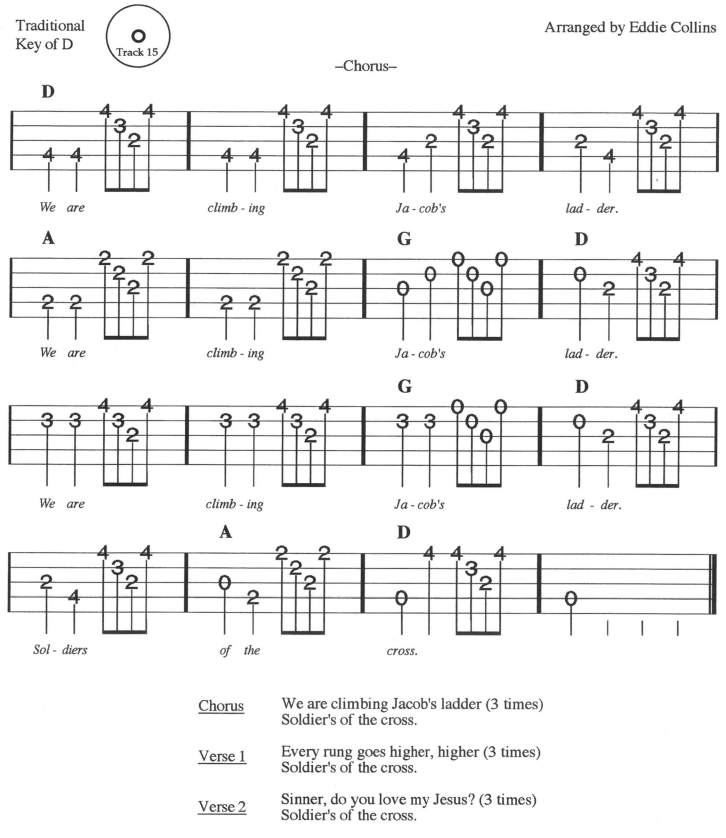

Chorus	We are climbing Jacob's ladder (3 times) Soldier's of the cross.
Verse 1	Every rung goes higher, higher (3 times) Soldier's of the cross.
Verse 2	Sinner, do you love my Jesus? (3 times) Soldier's of the cross.

Note: Hold the appropriate chord while adding the M I T M roll at the end of each measure. Some hymnals have this in 3/4 time, but 4/4 is better when trying to include banjo rolls.

Jesus, Savior, Pilot Me

Traditional
Key of G

Track 16

Arranged by Eddie Collins

–Verse–

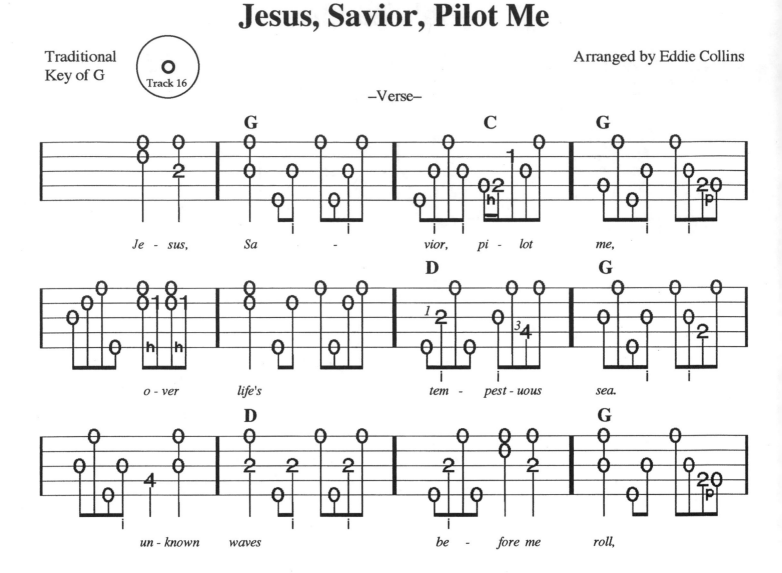

Je - sus,   Sa - vior, pi - lot me,

o - ver life's   tem - pest - uous sea.

un - known waves   be - fore me roll,

Verse 1
Jesus, Savior, pilot me,
Over life's tempestuous sea.
Unknown waves before me roll,
Hiding rock and treacherous shoal.
Chart and compass come from thee;
Jesus, Savior, pilot me.

Verse 2
As a mother stills her child,
Thou canst hush the ocean wild.
Boisterous waves obey thy will,
When thou says unto them, "Be still!"
Wondrous sovereign of the sea;
Jesus, Savior, pilot me.

Verse 3
When at last I near the shore,
And the fearful breakers roar.
'Twixt me and the peaceful rest,
Then, while leaning on thy breast;
May I hear thee say to me,
"Fear not, I will pilot thee."

Jesus, Savior, Pilot Me

Traditional
Key of G

Arranged by Eddie Collins

Track 16

–Verse Continued–

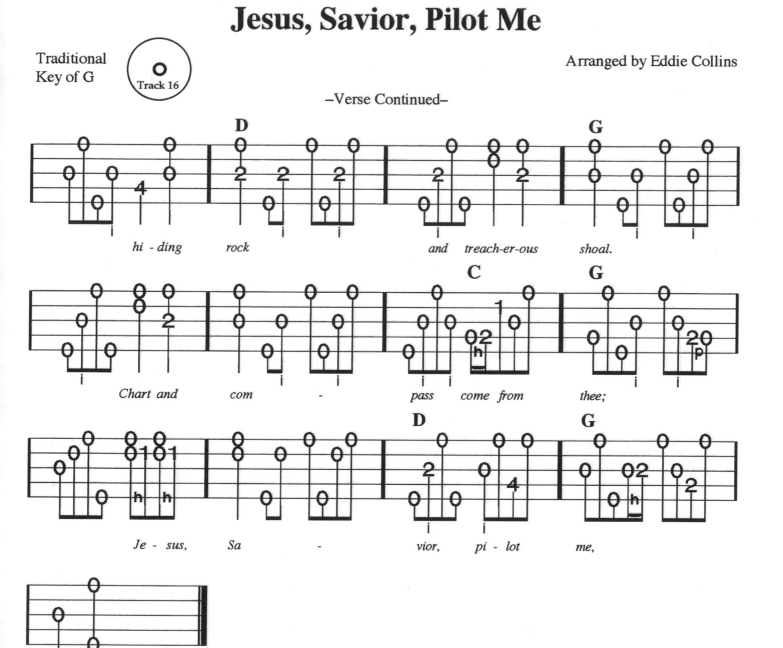

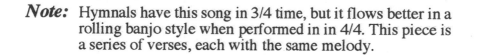

Note: Hymnals have this song in 3/4 time, but it flows better in a
rolling banjo style when performed in in 4/4. This piece is
a series of verses, each with the same melody.

Jesus Loves Me

Traditional
Key of C

Track 17

Arranged by Eddie Collins

–Verse–

Jes - sus loves me, this I know, for the Bi - ble tells me so.

Lit - tle ones to Him be - long; they are weak, but He is strong.

–Chorus–

Yes, Jes - sus loves me! Yes, Jes - sus loves me!

Yes, Jes - sus loves me! the Bi - ble tells me so.

Verse 1	Jesus loves me, this I know, for the Bible tells me so. Little ones to Him belong; they are weak, but He is strong.
Chorus	Yes, Jesus loves me! Yes, Jesus loves me! Yes, Jesus loves me! The Bible tells me so.
Verse 2	Jesus loves me, this I know, as He loved so long ago. Taking children on His knee, saying, "Let them come to me."
Verse 3	Jesus loves me still today, walking with me on my way. Wanting as a friend to give, light and love to all who live.
Verse 4	Jesus loves me, He who died, heaven's gate to open wide. He will wash away my sin, let His little child come in.
Verse 5	Jesus loves me, He will stay, close beside me all the way. Thou hast bled and died for me; I will henceforth live for Thee.
Verse 6	Jesus loves me, loves me still, though I'm very weak and ill. That I might from sin be free, bled and died upon the tree.

28

Joyful, Joyful, We Adore Thee

Traditional
Key of G

Track 18

Arranged by Eddie Collins

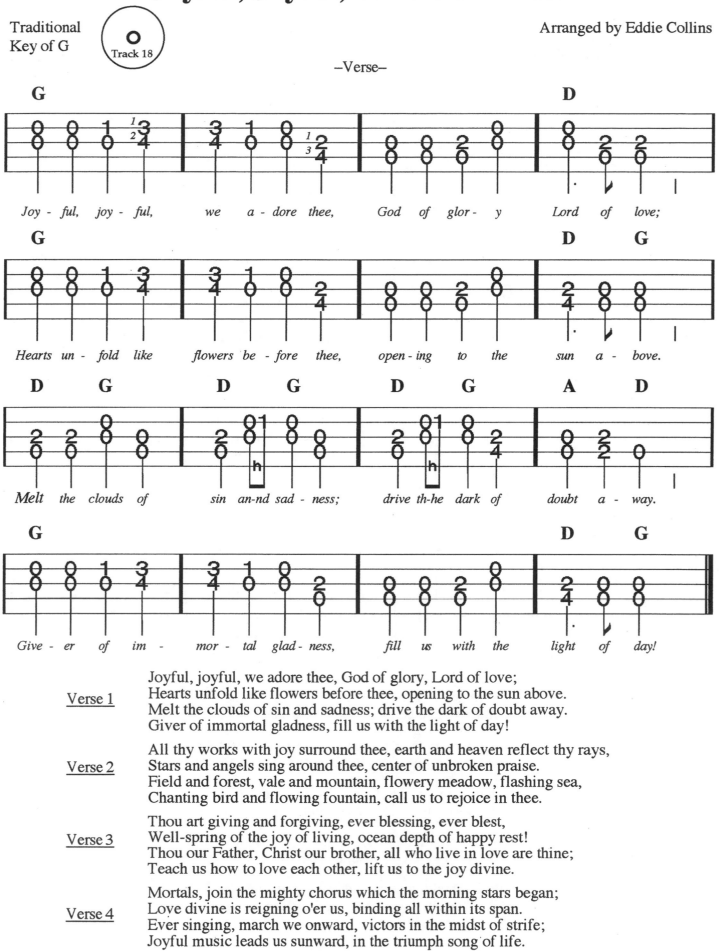

Verse 1
Joyful, joyful, we adore thee, God of glory, Lord of love;
Hearts unfold like flowers before thee, opening to the sun above.
Melt the clouds of sin and sadness; drive the dark of doubt away.
Giver of immortal gladness, fill us with the light of day!

Verse 2
All thy works with joy surround thee, earth and heaven reflect thy rays,
Stars and angels sing around thee, center of unbroken praise.
Field and forest, vale and mountain, flowery meadow, flashing sea,
Chanting bird and flowing fountain, call us to rejoice in thee.

Verse 3
Thou art giving and forgiving, ever blessing, ever blest,
Well-spring of the joy of living, ocean depth of happy rest!
Thou our Father, Christ our brother, all who live in love are thine;
Teach us how to love each other, lift us to the joy divine.

Verse 4
Mortals, join the mighty chorus which the morning stars began;
Love divine is reigning o'er us, binding all within its span.
Ever singing, march we onward, victors in the midst of strife;
Joyful music leads us sunward, in the triumph song of life.

Just Over In The Glory Land

Traditional
Key of G

Track 19

Arranged by Eddie Collins

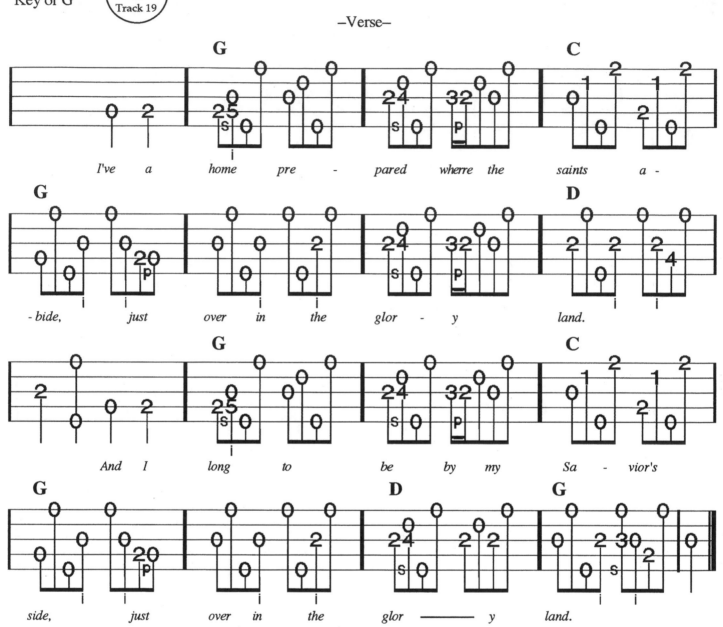

Verse 1 — I've a home prepared where the saints abide, *
And I long to be by my Saviour's side, *

Chorus — Just over in the glory land, I'll join the happy angel band, *
Just over in the glory land, there with the mighty host I'll stand, *

Verse 2 — I am on my way to those mansions fair, *
There to sing God's praises and his glory share, *

Verse 3 — What a joyful thought that my Lord I'll see, *
And with kindred saved, there forever be, *

Verse 4 — With the blood washed throng I will shout and sing, *
Glad hosannas to Christ, the Lord and King, *

*Insert the lyric "Just over in the glory land," after each line of each verse and chorus.

Just Over In The Glory Land

Traditional
Key of G

Track 19

Arranged by Eddie Collins

—Chorus—

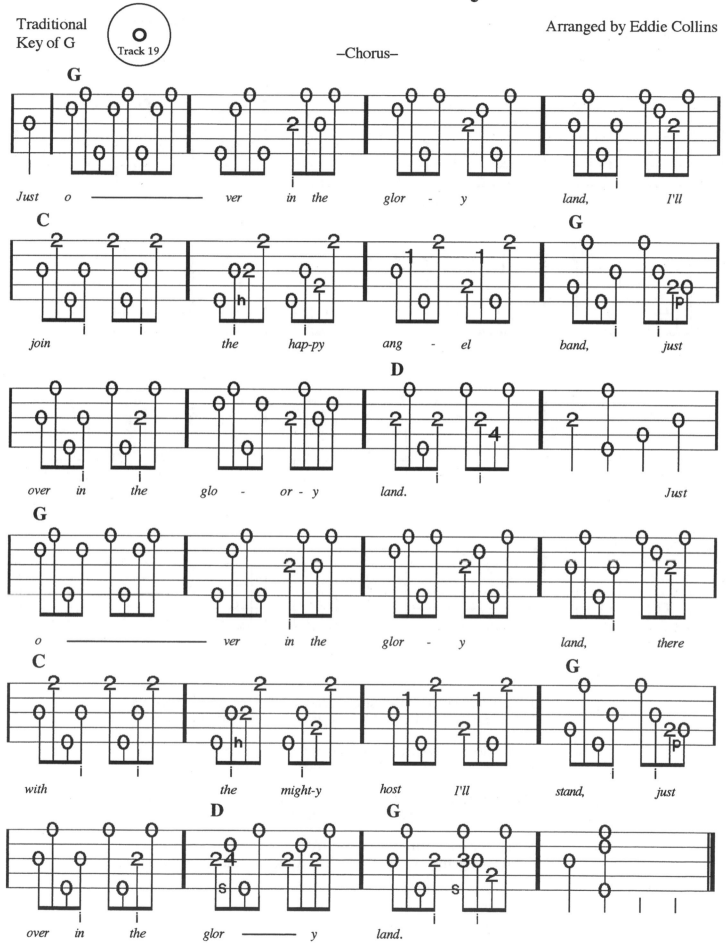

31

Just A Closer Walk With Thee

Traditional
Key of C

Track 20

Arranged by Eddie Collins

–Chorus–

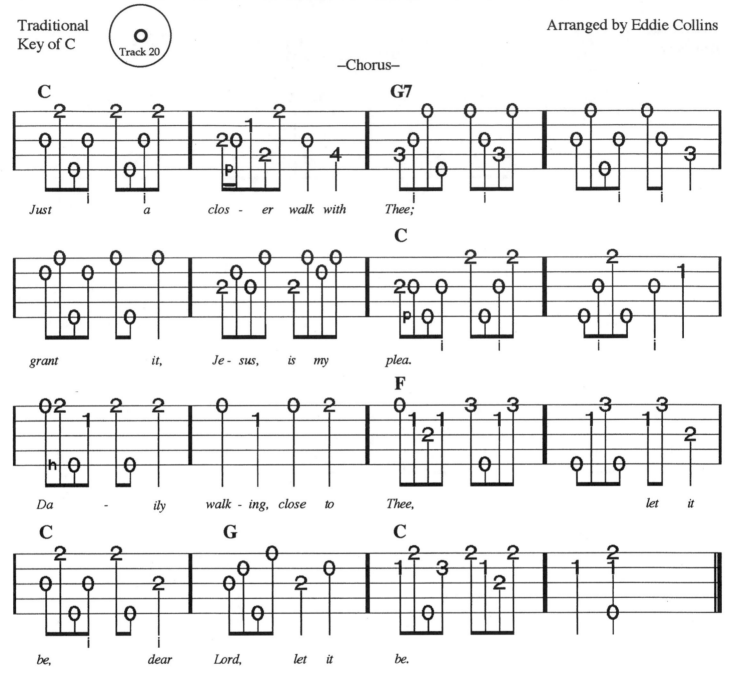

Verse 1   I am weak, but Thou art strong; Jesus, keep me from all wrong.
           I'll be satisfied as long as I walk, let me walk close to Thee.

Chorus   Just a closer walk with Thee, grant it, Jesus, is my plea.
           Daily walking close to Thee, let it be, dear Lord, let it be.

Verse 2   Through this world of toil and snares, if I falter, Lord, who cares?
           Who with me my burden shares? None but Thee, dear Lord, none but Thee.

Verse 3   When my feeble life is o'er, time for me will be no more;
           Guide me gently, safely o'er to Thy kingdom shore, to Thy shore.

Note: All verses share the same melody as the chorus.

Keep Your Lamp Trimmed And Burning

Traditional
Key of G

Track 21

Arranged by Eddie Collins

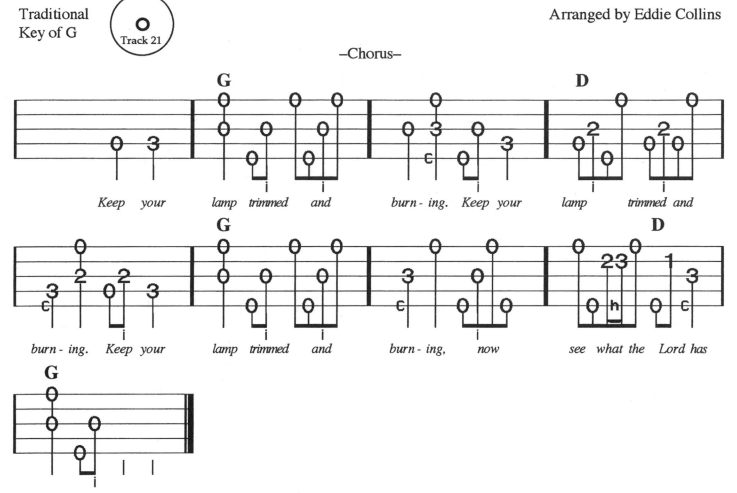

–Chorus–

Keep your lamp trimmed and burn-ing. Keep your lamp trimmed and burn-ing. Keep your lamp trimmed and burn-ing, now see what the Lord has done.

Verse 1	Troubles and trials are almost over (3 times) Now see what the Lord has done.	
Chorus	Keep your lamp trimmed and burning (3 times) Now see what the Lord has done.	
Verse 2	Heaven's journey is going on stronger (3 times) Now see what the Lord has done.	
Verse 3	Brother don't you worry (3 times) Now see what the Lord has done.	
Verse 4	Sister don't stop praying (3 times) Now see what the Lord has done.	
Verse 5	Many are gone, but not forgotten (3 times) Now see what the Lord has done.	

Note: All verses share the same melody as the chorus.

Keep On The Sunny Side

Traditional
Key of G

Arranged by Eddie Collins

–Verse–

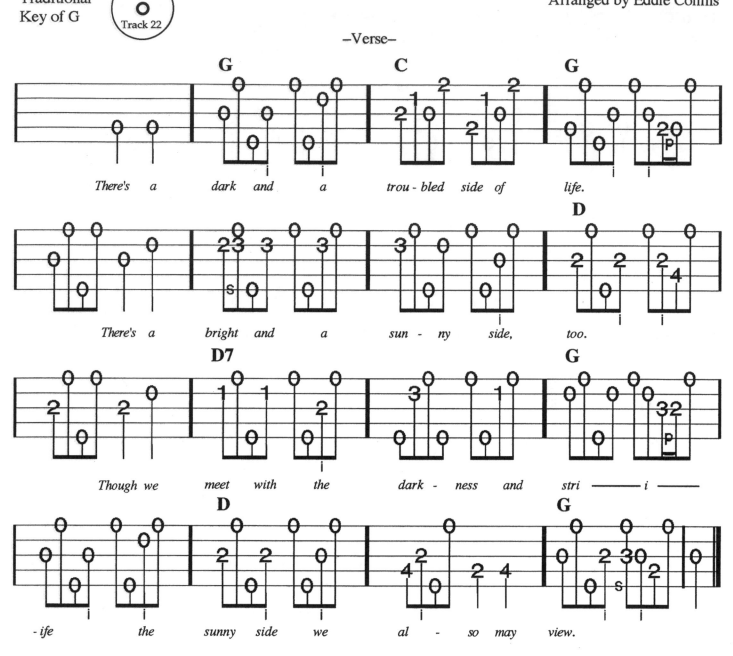

Verse 1

There's a dark and a troubled side of life.
There's a bright and a sunny side, too.
Though we meet with the darkness and strife,
The sunny side we also may view.

Verse 2

Oh, the storm and its fury broke today.
Crushing hopes that we cherish so dear.
The clouds and storm will in time pass away.
The sun again will shine bright and clear.

Keep On The Sunny Side

Traditional
Key of G

Arranged by Eddie Collins

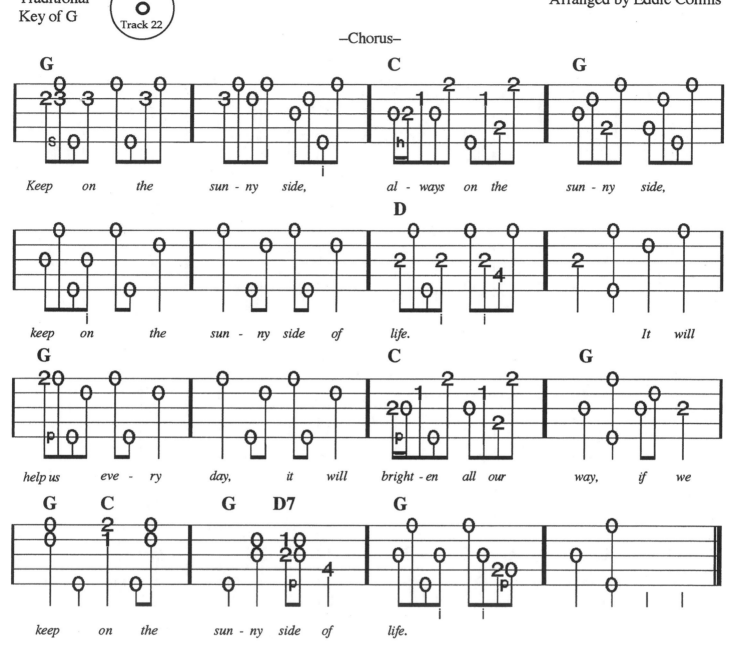

Chorus

Keep on the sunny side, always on the sunny side,
Keep on the sunny side of life.
It will help us every day; it will brighten all our way,
If we keep on the sunny side of life.

Verse 3

Let us greet with a song of hope each day,
Though the moment be cloudy or fair.
Let us trust in our Savior always,
To keep us every one in His care.

Note: Perform all the two-string pinches on strings 1, 2 and 3 with I and M.

Leaning On The Everlasting Arms

Traditional
Key of G

Track 23

Arranged by Eddie Collins

–Verse–

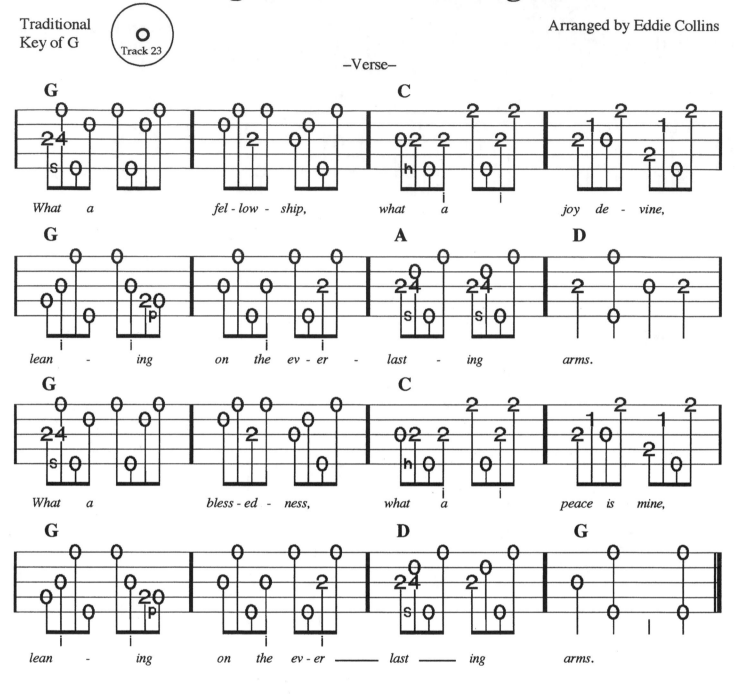

Verse 1
What a fellowship, what a joy divine,
leaning on the everlasting arms.
What a blessedness, what a peace is mine,
leaning on the everlasting arms.

Verse 2
O how sweet to walk in this pilgrim way,
leaning on the everlasting arms.
O how bright the path grows from day to day,
leaning on the everlasting arms.

Leaning On The Everlasting Arms

Traditional
Key of G

Track 23

Arranged by Eddie Collins

–Chorus–

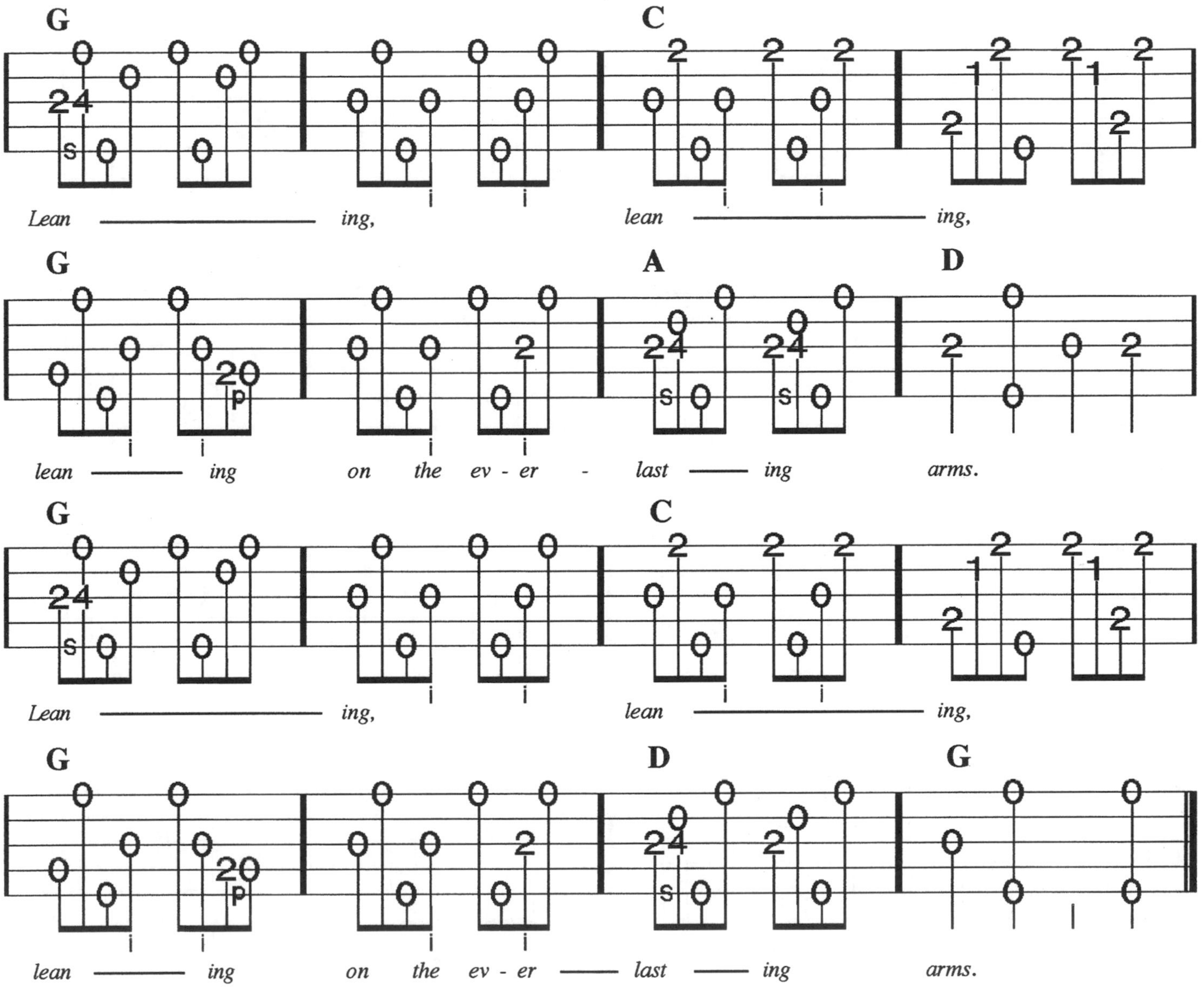

Lean ————— ing, lean ————— ing,

lean ——— ing on the ev - er - last ——— ing arms.

Lean ————— ing, lean ————— ing,

lean ——— ing on the ev - er ——— last ——— ing arms.

Chorus
Leaning, leaning, safe and secure from all alarms.
Leaning, leaning, leaning on the everlasting arms.

Verse 3
What have I to dread, what have I to fear,
leaning on the everlasting arms?
I have blessed peace with my Lord so near,
leaning on the everlasting arms.

37

Let Me Rest At The End Of My Journey

Traditional
Key of G

Track 24

Arranged by Eddie Collins

–Verse–

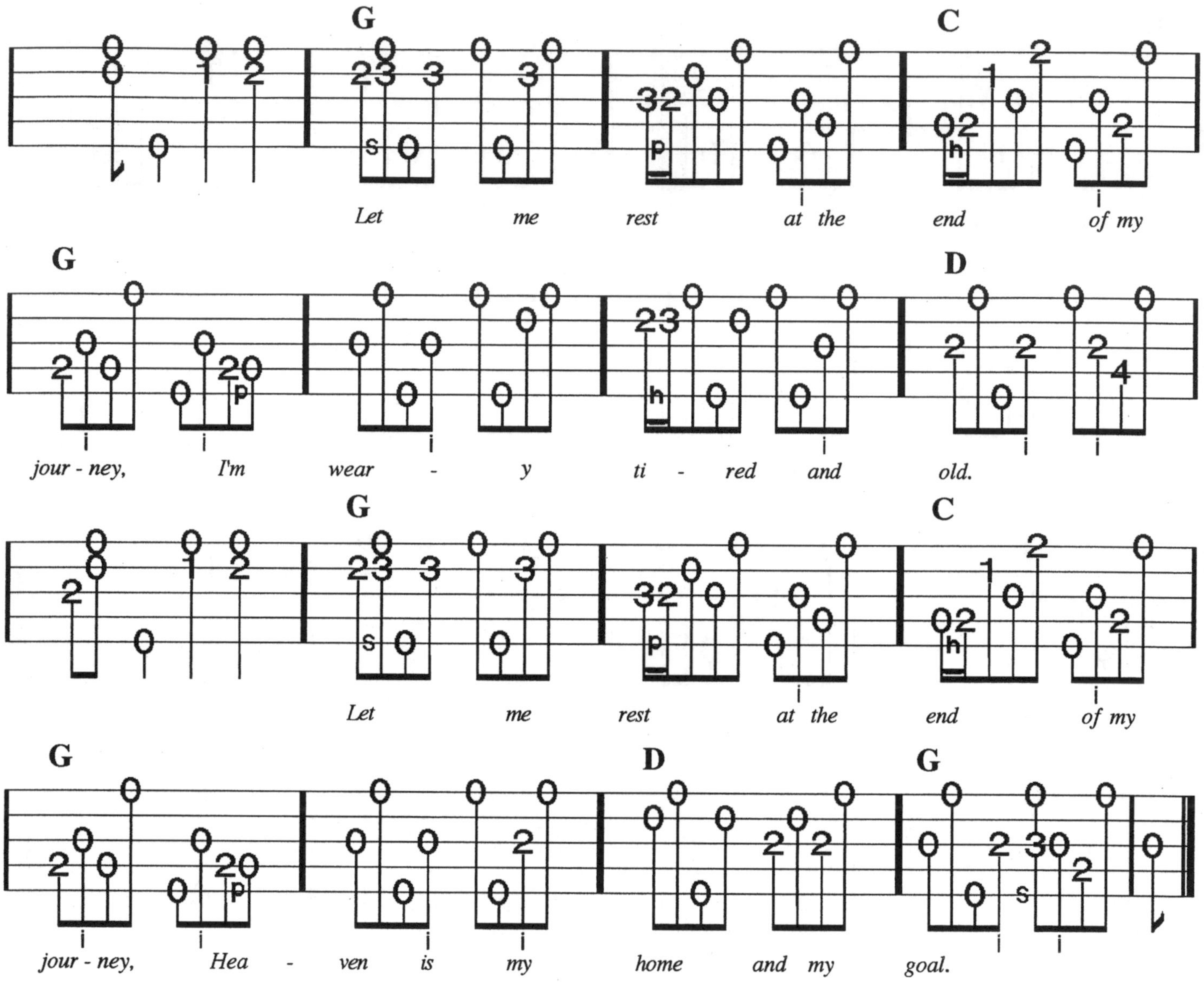

Let me rest at the end of my jour-ney, I'm wear-y ti-red and old. Let me rest at the end of my jour-ney, Hea-ven is my home and my goal.

Verse 1
Let me rest at the end of my journey,
I'm weary, tired, and old.
Let me rest at the end of my journey,
Heaven is my home and my goal.

Verse 2
A cowboy's life on the old Texas trail,
Herding doggies is all that he knows.
A cowboy's life on the old cattle trail,
Leads from Texas to old Mexico.

Let Me Rest At The End Of My Journey

Traditional
Key of G

Track 24

Arranged by Eddie Collins

–Chorus–

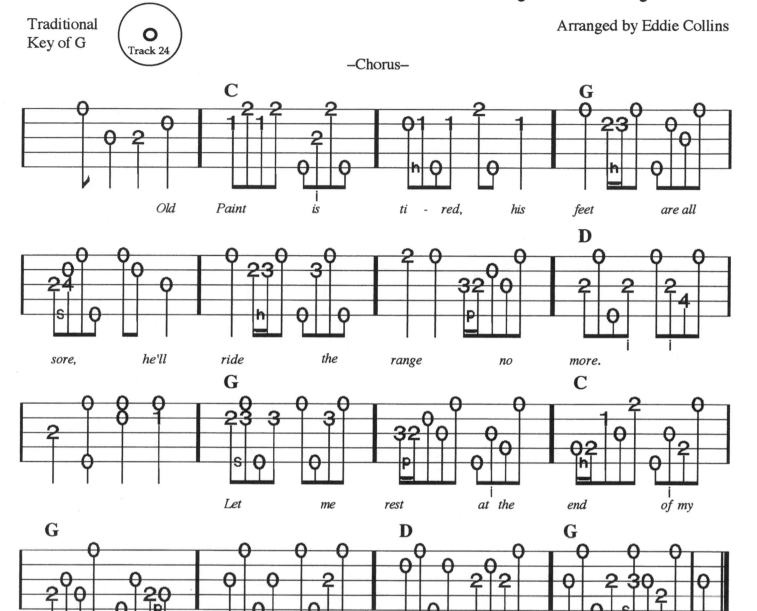

Old Paint is ti - red, his feet are all sore, he'll ride the range no more.

Let me rest at the end of my jour - ney, Hea - ven is my home and my goal.

Chorus

Old paint is tired, his feet are all sore,
We'll ride the range no more.
Let me rest at the end of my journey,
Heaven is my home and my goal.

Let The Church Roll On

Traditional
Key of G

Track 25

Arranged by Eddie Collins

–Chorus and Verse–

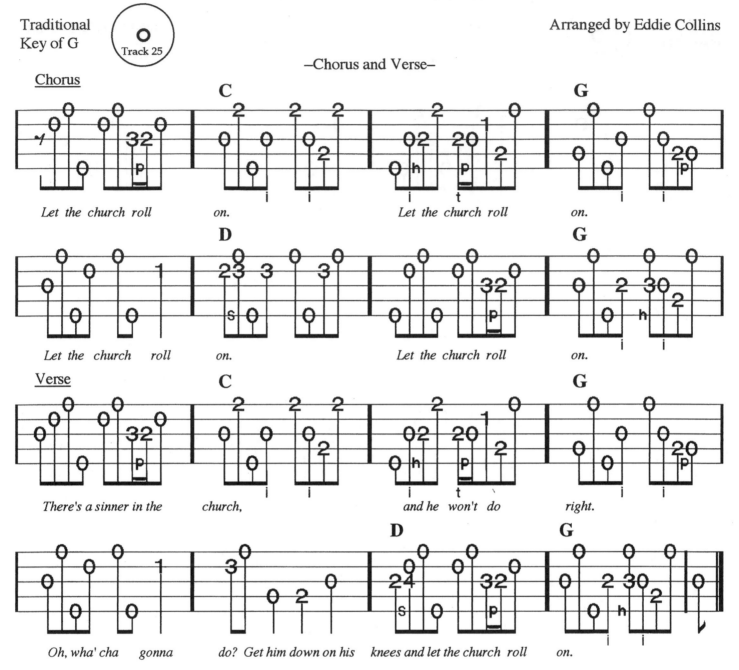

Chorus

Let the church roll on. Let the church roll on.
Let the church roll on. Let the church roll on.

Verse

There's a sinner in the church, and he won't do right.
Oh, wha' cha gonna do? Get him down on his knees and let the church roll on.

Chorus   Let the church roll on. (4 times).

Verse 1   There's a sinner in the church and he won't do right.
Wha'cha gonna do? Get him down on his knees and let the church roll on.

Verse 2   There's a deacon in the church and he won't do right.
Wha'cha gonna do? Take his name off the roll and let the church roll on.

Verse 3   There's a preacher in the church and he won't do right.
Wha'cha gonna do? Kick him out, kick him out! And let the church roll on.

Verse 4   There's a drunkard in the church and he won't do right.
Wha'cha gonna do? Take away his liquor and let the church roll on.

No Hiding Place Down Here

Traditional
Key of G

Track 27

Arranged by Eddie Collins

–Chorus–

Verse 1
Sister Mary, she wears a golden chain. (3 times)
On every link there's Jesus name. There's no hiding place down here.

Chorus
There's no hiding place down here. (2 times)
Well, I run to the rocks and I hide my face;
The rocks cried out, no hiding place. There's no hiding place down here.

Verse 2
I'll pitch my tent on the old camp ground. (3 times)
I'll give old Satan one more round. There's no hiding place down here.

Verse 3
Oh, the devil, he wears a hypocrite's shoe. (3 times)
If you don't watch, he'll slip it on you. There's no hiding place down here.

Note: All verses share the same melody as the chorus.

41

Old Time Religion

Traditional
Key of G

Track 29

Arranged by Eddie Collins

–Chorus–

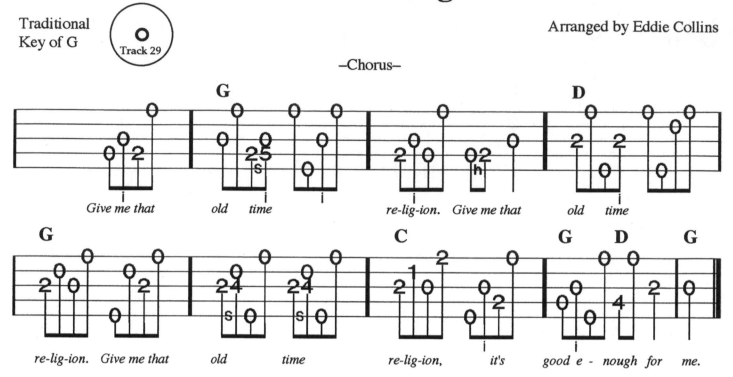

Give me that old time re-lig-ion. Give me that old time re-lig-ion. Give me that old time re-lig-ion, it's good e - nough for me.

Chorus	Give me that old time religion, Give me that old time religion. Give me that old time religion, It's good enough for me.
Verse 1	It was good for the Hebrew children (3 times) It's good enough for me.
Verse 2	It was tried in the fiery furnace (3 times) It's good enough for me.
Verse 3	It will do when I am dying (3 times) It's good enough for me.
Verse 4	It will take us all up to heaven (3 times) It's good enough for me.

Note: All verses share the same melody as the chorus.

Peace Like A River

Traditional
Key of G

Track 31

Arranged by Eddie Collins

–Verse–

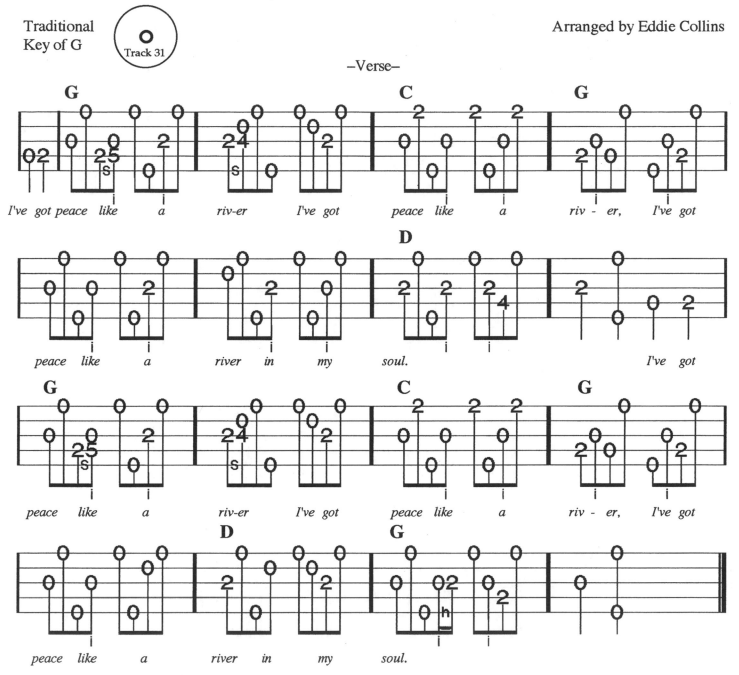

Verse 1
I've got peace like a river, I've got peace like a river,
I've got peace like a river, in my soul.
I've got peace like a river, I've got peace like a river,
I've got peace like a river, in my soul.

Verse 2
I've got joy like a fountain, (etc.)

Verse 3
I've got love like the ocean, (etc.)

Note: This song is a series of verses, each with the same melody.

Pass Me Not O Gentle Savior

Traditional
Key of G

Arranged by Eddie Collins

Track 32

—Verse—

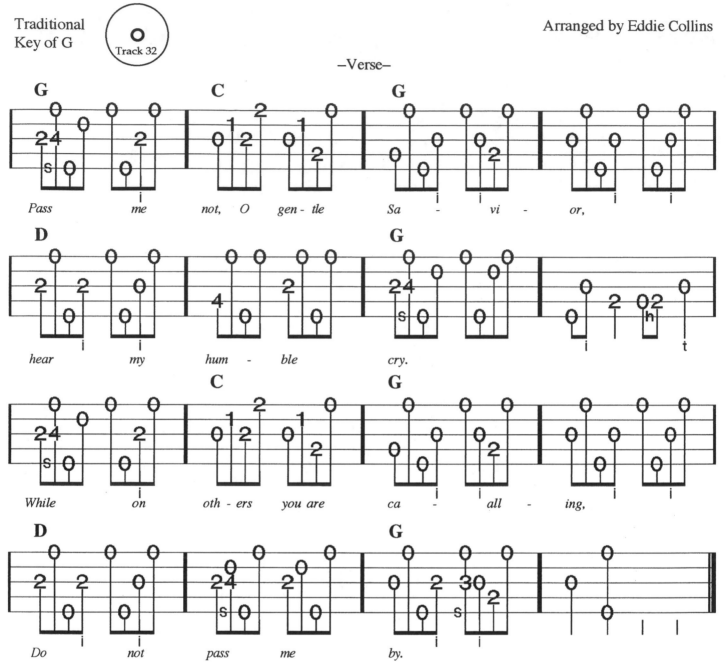

Pass	me	not, O gen - tle	Sa - vi - or,		

hear my hum - ble cry.

While on oth - ers you are ca - all - ing,

Do not pass me by.

<u>Verse 1</u>   Pass me not, O gentle Savior, hear my humble cry.
                  While on others thou art calling, do not pass me by.

<u>Verse 2</u>   Let me at thy throne of mercy, find a sweet relief;
                  Kneeling there in deep contrition; help my unbelief.

<u>Verse 3</u>   Trusting only in Thy merit, would I seek Thy face.
                  Heal my wounded, broken spirit, save me by Thy grace.

Pass Me Not O Gentle Savior

Traditional
Key of G

Track 32

Arranged by Eddie Collins

–Chorus–

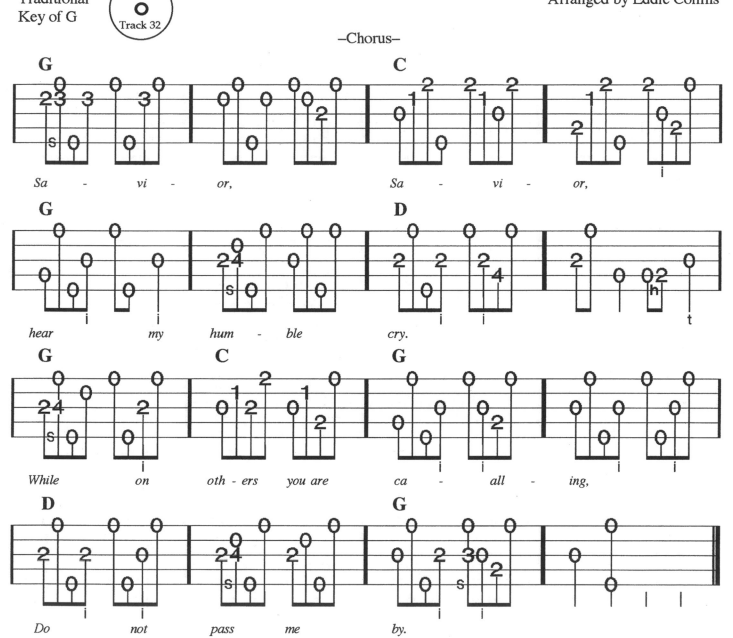

Chorus   Savior, Savior, hear my humble cry;
While on others thou art calling, do not pass me by.

Verse 4   Thou the spring of all my comfort, more than life to me.
Whom have I on earth beside Thee? Whom in heaven but Thee?

Softly And Tenderly

Traditional
Key of G

Track 33

Arranged by Eddie Collins

–Verse–

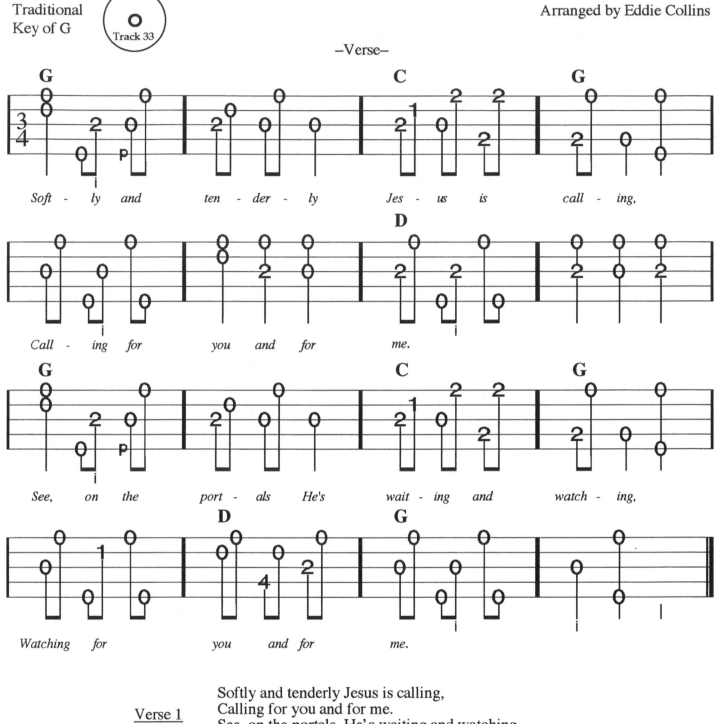

Softly and tenderly Jesus is calling,
Calling for you and for me.
See, on the portals, He's waiting and watching,
Watching for you and for me.

Verse 1

Come home, come home,
You who are weary, come home.
Earnestly, tenderly, Jesus is calling,
Calling, O sinner, come home!

Chorus

Softly And Tenderly

Traditional
Key of G

Track 33

Arranged by Eddie Collins

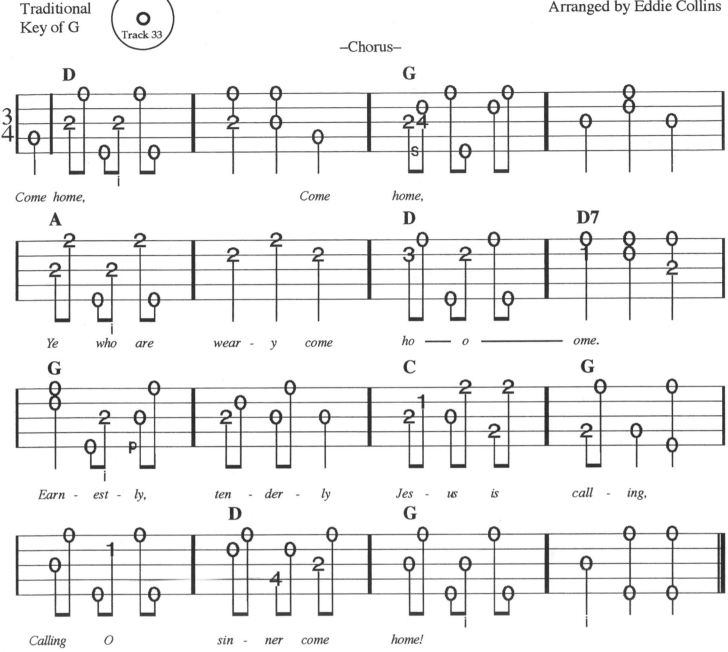

Come home, Come home, Ye who are wear-y come ho — o — ome. Earn-est-ly, ten-der-ly Jes-us is call-ing, Calling O sin-ner come home!

Verse 2

Why should we tarry when Jesus is pleading,
Pleading for you and for me?
Why should we linger and heed not His mercies,
Mercies for you and for me?

Verse 3

Time is now fleeting, the moments are passing,
Passing from you and from me.
Shadows are gathering, deathbeds are coming,
Coming for you and for me.

Verse 4

Oh, for the wonderful love He has promised,
Promised for you and for me.
Though we have sinned, He has mercy and pardon,
Pardon for you and for me.

Somebody Touched Me

Traditional
Key of G
Track 34

Arranged by Eddie Collins

–Verse–

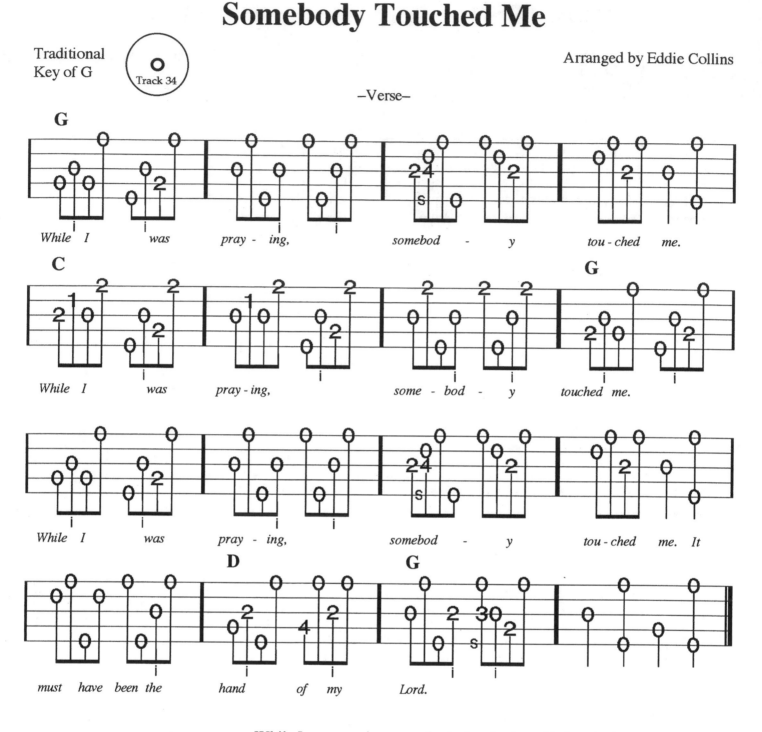

Verse 1
While I was praying, somebody touched me (3 times)
It must have been the hand of my Lord.

Verse 2
Glory, glory, glory, somebody touched me (3 times)
It must have been the hand of my Lord.

Verse 3
While I was singing, somebody touched me (3 times)
It must have been the hand of my Lord.

Verse 4
While I was preaching, somebody touched me (3 times)
It must have been the hand of my Lord.

Note: This song is a series of verses, all with the same melody.

Standing On The Promises

Traditional
Key of G

Track 36

Arranged by Eddie Collins

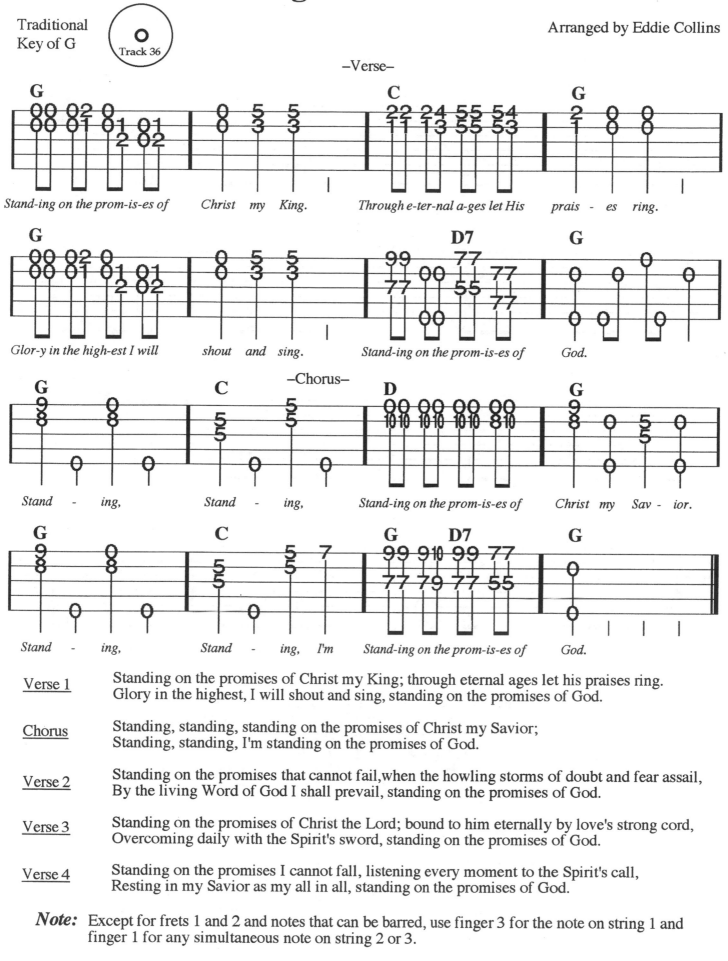

Verse 1   Standing on the promises of Christ my King; through eternal ages let his praises ring. Glory in the highest, I will shout and sing, standing on the promises of God.

Chorus   Standing, standing, standing on the promises of Christ my Savior; Standing, standing, I'm standing on the promises of God.

Verse 2   Standing on the promises that cannot fail, when the howling storms of doubt and fear assail, By the living Word of God I shall prevail, standing on the promises of God.

Verse 3   Standing on the promises of Christ the Lord; bound to him eternally by love's strong cord, Overcoming daily with the Spirit's sword, standing on the promises of God.

Verse 4   Standing on the promises I cannot fall, listening every moment to the Spirit's call, Resting in my Savior as my all in all, standing on the promises of God.

Note: Except for frets 1 and 2 and notes that can be barred, use finger 3 for the note on string 1 and finger 1 for any simultaneous note on string 2 or 3.

'Tis So Sweet To Trust In Jesus

Traditional
Key of G

Track 37

Arranged by Eddie Collins

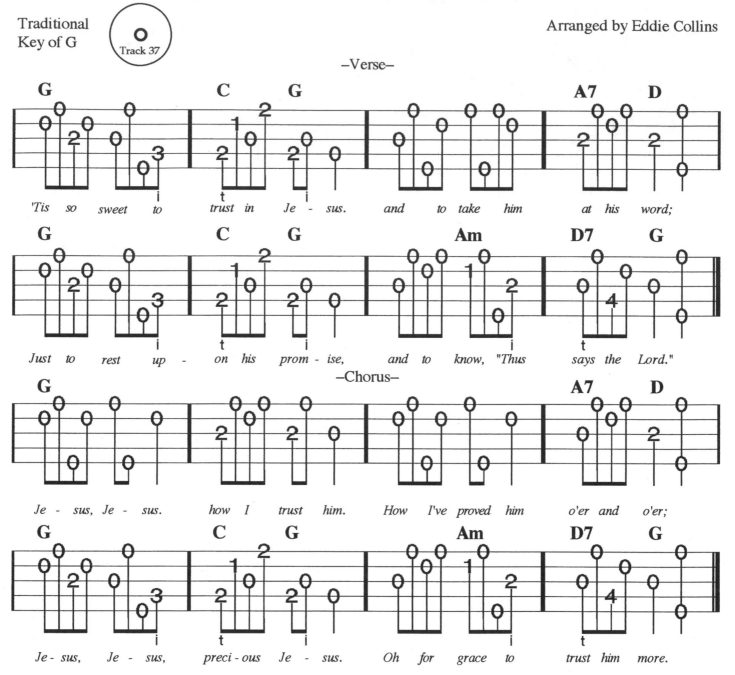

Verse 1   'Tis so sweet to trust in Jesus, and to take him at his word;
Just to rest upon his promise, and to know, "Thus says the Lord."

Chorus   Jesus, Jesus, how I trust him. How I've proved him o'er and o'er;
Jesus, Jesus, precious Jesus. Oh for grace to trust him more.

Verse 2   Oh how sweet to trust in Jesus, just to trust his cleansing blood;
And in simple faith to plunge me, 'neath the healing, cleansing flood.

Verse 3   Yes, 'tis sweet to trust in Jesus, just from sin and self to cease;
Just from Jesus simply taking life and rest, and joy and peace.

Verse 4   I'm so glad I learned to trust thee, precious Jesus, Savior, friend;
And I know that thou art with me, and will be until the end.

This Little Light Of Mine

Traditional
Key of G

Track 38

Arranged by Eddie Collins

–Chorus–

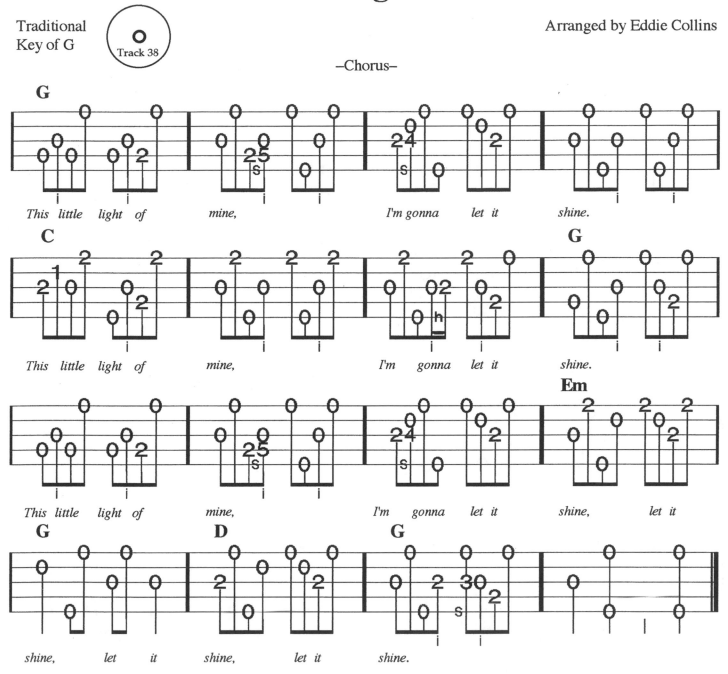

Chorus	This little light of mine, I'm gonna let it shine. (3 times) Let it shine, let it shine, let it shine.
Verse 1	Hide it under a bushel? No! I'm gonna let it shine. (3 times) Let it shine, let it shine, let it shine.
Verse 2	Won't let Satan blow it out, I'm gonna let it shine. (3 times) Let it shine, let it shine, let it shine.
Verse 3	Let it shine til Jesus comes, I'm gonna let it shine. (3 times) Let it shine, let it shine, let it shine.

Note: All verses share the same melody as the chorus.

Wayfaring Stranger

Traditional
Key of A minor

Track 40

Arranged by Eddie Collins

–Verse–

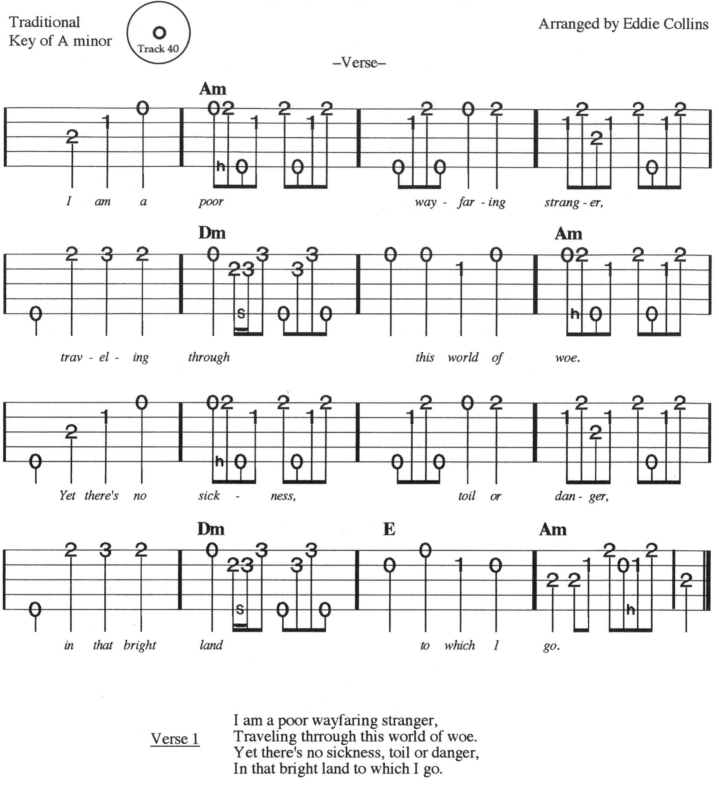

Verse 1
I am a poor wayfaring stranger,
Traveling thrrough this world of woe.
Yet there's no sickness, toil or danger,
In that bright land to which I go.

Verse 2
I know dark clouds will gather 'round me;
I know my way is rough and steep.
Yet beauteous fields, lie just before me,
Where God's redeemed, their vigils keep.

Wayfaring Stranger

Traditional
Key of A minor

Track 40

Arranged by Eddie Collins

–Bridge–

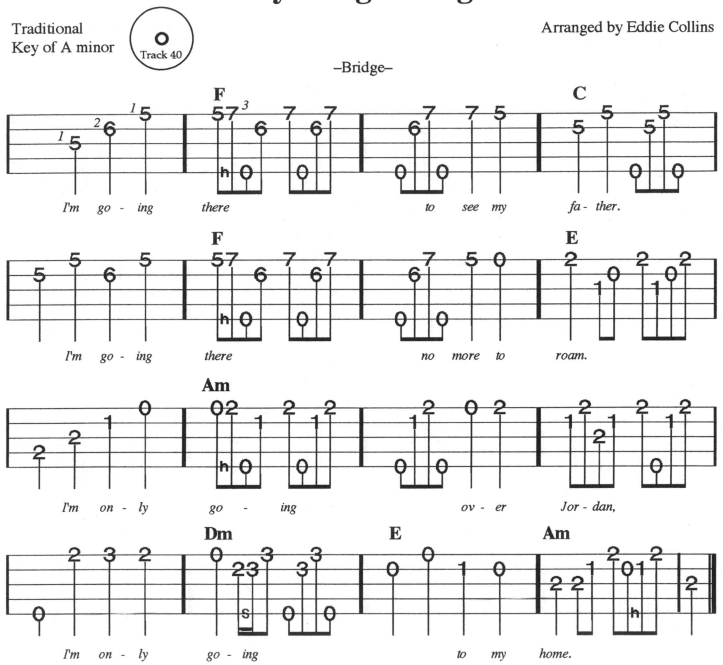

Bridge 1
I'm going there to see my father,
I'm going there no more to roam.
I'm only going over Jordan,
I'm only going to my home.

Bridge 2
I'm going there to see my mother,
She said she'd meet me when I come.
I'm only going over Jordan,
I'm only going to my home.

What A Friend We Have In Jesus

Traditional
Key of G

Track 41

Arranged by Eddie Collins

–First Half of Verse–

What a friend we have in Je ——————— sus,

all our sins and griefs to bear.

What a priv - i - lege to car ——————— ry,

ev - er - y - thing to God in prayer.

Verse 1
What a friend we have in Jesus, all our sins and griefs to bear.
What a privilege to carry, everything to God in prayer.
Oh, what peace we often forfeit, oh, what needless pain we bear,
All because we do not carry, everything to God in prayer.

Verse 2
Have we trials and temptations? Is there trouble anywhere?
We should never be discouraged, take it to the Lord in prayer.
Can we find a friend so faithful, who will all our sorrows share?
Jesus knows our every weakness; take it to the Lord in prayer.

What A Friend We Have In Jesus

Traditional
Key of G

Track 41

Arranged by Eddie Collins

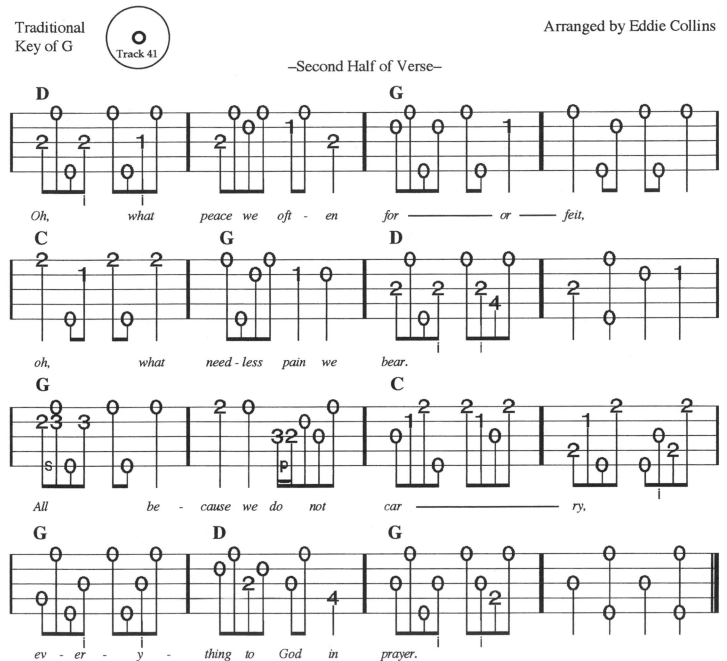

Verse 3
Are we weak and heavy laden, cumbered with a load of care?
Precious Savior, still our refuge; take it to the Lord in prayer.
Do thy friends despise, forsake thee? Take it to the Lord in prayer.
In His arms He'll take and shield thee; Thou wilt find a solace there.

Verse 4
Blessed Savior, Thou hast promised, Thou wilt all our burdens bear;
May we ever, Lord, be bringing, all to Thee in earnest prayer.
Soon in glory bright, unclouded, there will be no need for prayer.
Rapture, praise, and endless worship, will be our sweet portion there.

What Would You Give In Exchange For Your Soul?

Traditional
Key of G

Track 42

Arranged by Eddie Collins

–First Half of Chorus–

*Verse 1
Brother afar from the Savior today,
Risking your soul for the things that decay,
Oh, if today God should call it away,
What would you give in exchange for your soul?

Chorus
What would you give? What would you give?
What would you give in exchange for your soul?
Oh, if today God should call it away,
What would you give in exchange for your soul?

Verse 2
Mercy is calling you, won't you give heed?
Must the dear Savior still tenderly plead?
Risk not your soul, it is precious indeed;
What would you give in exchange for your soul?

*The melody of the first two lines of each verse is slightly different than that of the chorus.

What Would You Give In Exchange For Your Soul?

Traditional
Key of G

Track 42

Arranged by Eddie Collins

–Chorus (continued)–

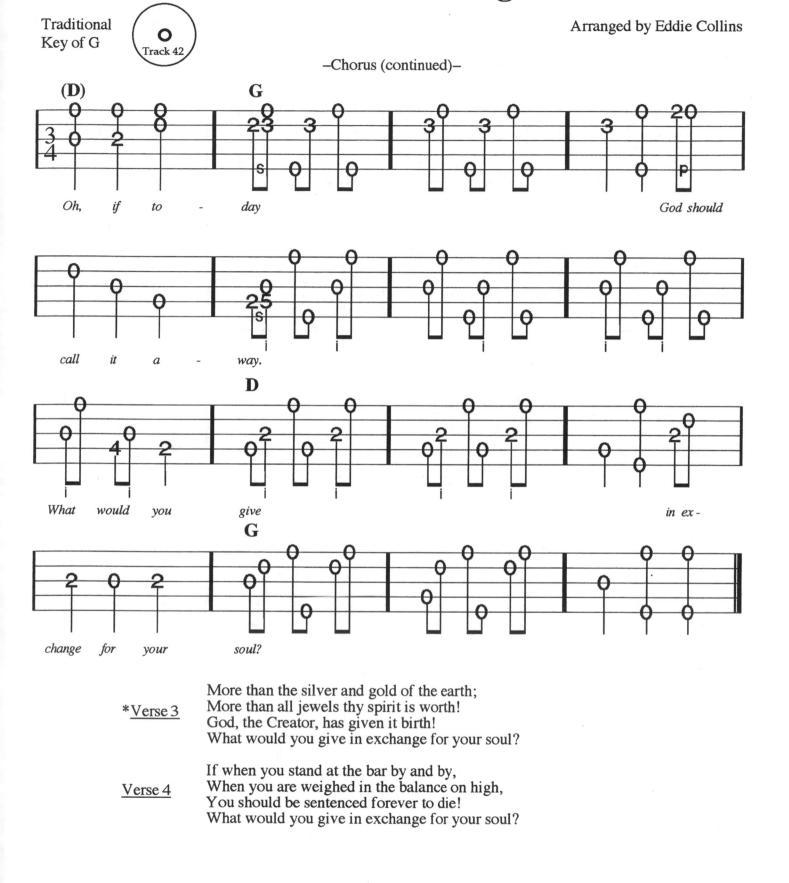

Oh, if to - day ... God should

call it a - way.

What would you give ... in ex-

change for your soul?

*Verse 3

More than the silver and gold of the earth;
More than all jewels thy spirit is worth!
God, the Creator, has given it birth!
What would you give in exchange for your soul?

Verse 4

If when you stand at the bar by and by,
When you are weighed in the balance on high,
You should be sentenced forever to die!
What would you give in exchange for your soul?

*The melody of the first two lines of each verse is slightly different than that of the chorus.

When The Roll Is Called Up Yonder

Traditional
Key of G

Track 43

Arranged by Eddie Collins

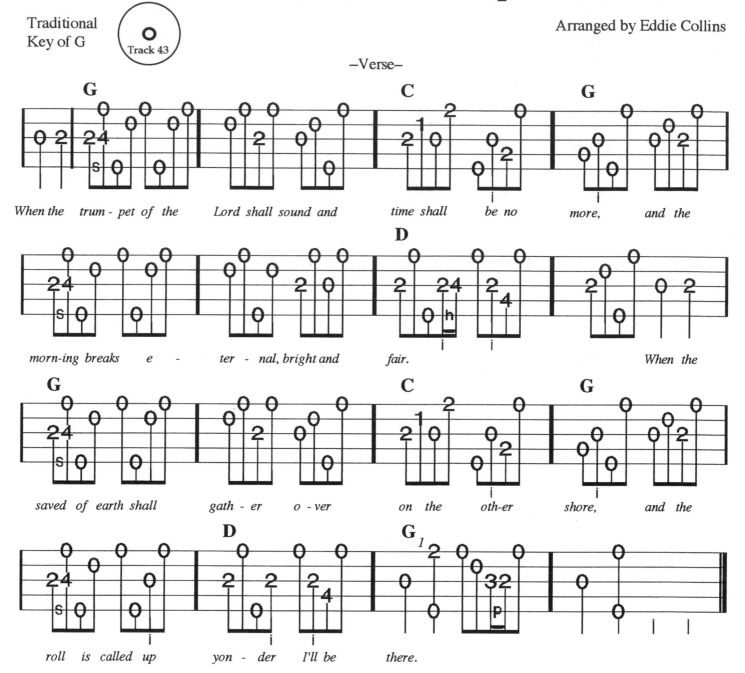

Verse 1

When the trumpet of the Lord shall sound and time shall be no more,
And the morning breaks eternal, bright and fair.
When the saved on earth shall gather over on the other shore,
And the roll is called up yonder I'll be there.

Verse 2

On that bright and cloudless morning when the dead in Christ shall rise,
And the glory of His resurrection share.
When His chosen ones shall gather to their home beyond the skies,
And the roll is called up yonder I'll be there.

When The Roll Is Called Up Yonder

Traditional
Key of G

Track 43

Arranged by Eddie Collins

–Chorus–

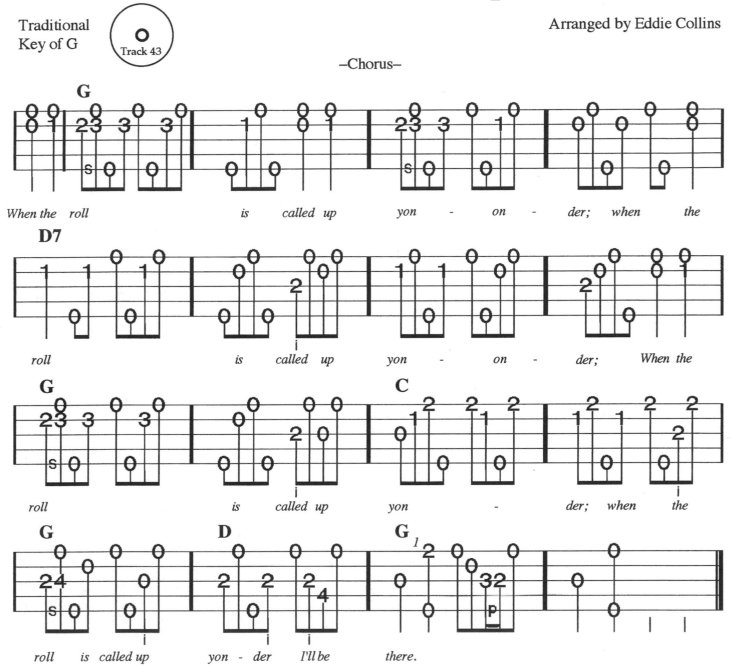

Chorus

When the roll is called up yonder;
When the roll is called up yonder.
When the roll is called up yonder;
When the roll is called up yonder, I'll be there.

Verse 3

Let us labor for the Master from the dawn til setting sun,
Let us talk of all His wondrous love and care.
Then when all of life is over and our work on earth is done,
And the roll is called up yonder I'll be there.

When The Saints Go Marching In

Traditional
Key of G

Arranged by Eddie Collins

Track 44

–Chorus–

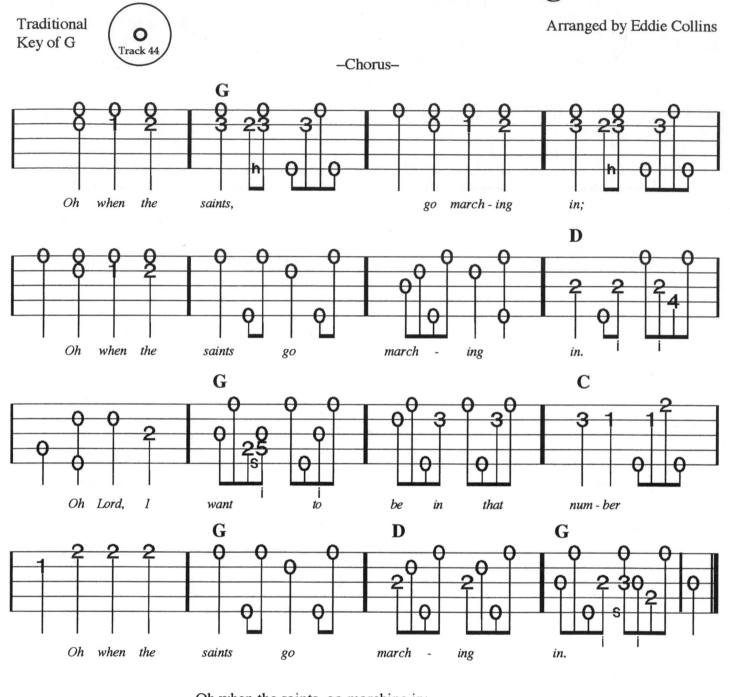

Chorus

Oh when the saints, go marching in;
Oh when the saints go marching in.
Oh Lord, I want to be in that number,
Oh when the saints go marching in.

Verse 1   Oh when the sun, refuses to shine.

Verse 2   Oh when the moon, turns red with blood.

Verse 3   Oh when the trumpet, sounds the call.

Note: There are too many versions of this song to claim one "correct" set of lyrics. Some versions begin with a verse that has a slightly different melody than the famous chorus. All of the above verses share the melody and follow the pattern of the chorus, where lines 1, 2 and 4 are the same with the third line being "Oh Lord, I want to be in that number."

When The Sun Of My Life Goes Down

Traditional
Key of G

Track 46

Arranged by Eddie Collins

—Verse—

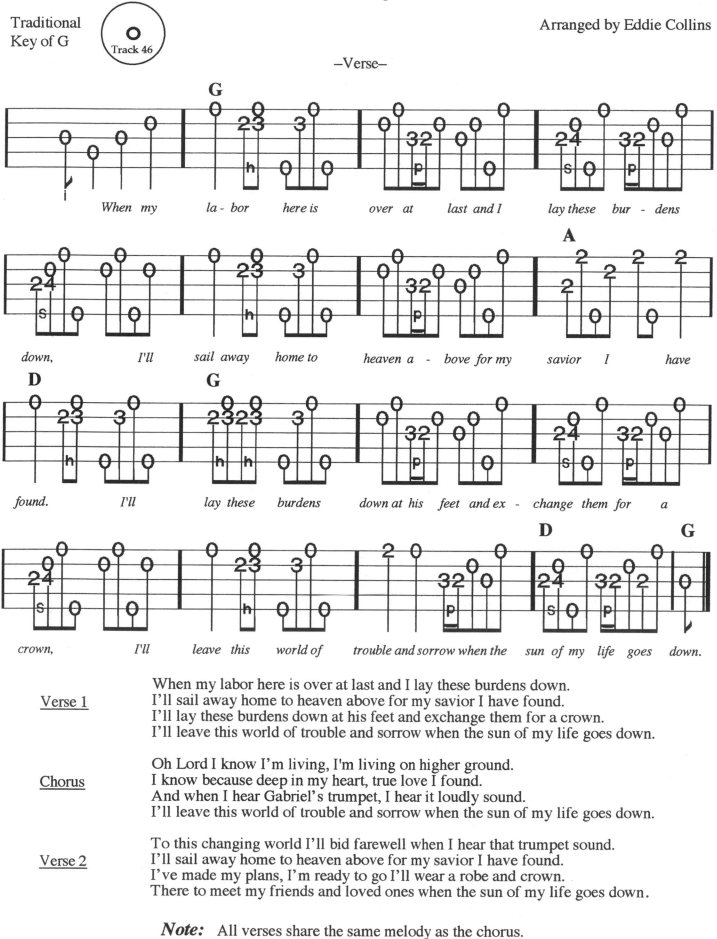

Verse 1
When my labor here is over at last and I lay these burdens down.
I'll sail away home to heaven above for my savior I have found.
I'll lay these burdens down at his feet and exchange them for a crown.
I'll leave this world of trouble and sorrow when the sun of my life goes down.

Chorus
Oh Lord I know I'm living, I'm living on higher ground.
I know because deep in my heart, true love I found.
And when I hear Gabriel's trumpet, I hear it loudly sound.
I'll leave this world of trouble and sorrow when the sun of my life goes down.

Verse 2
To this changing world I'll bid farewell when I hear that trumpet sound.
I'll sail away home to heaven above for my savior I have found.
I've made my plans, I'm ready to go I'll wear a robe and crown.
There to meet my friends and loved ones when the sun of my life goes down.

Note: All verses share the same melody as the chorus.

We Shall Overcome

Traditional
Key of G

Track 47

Arranged by Eddie Collins

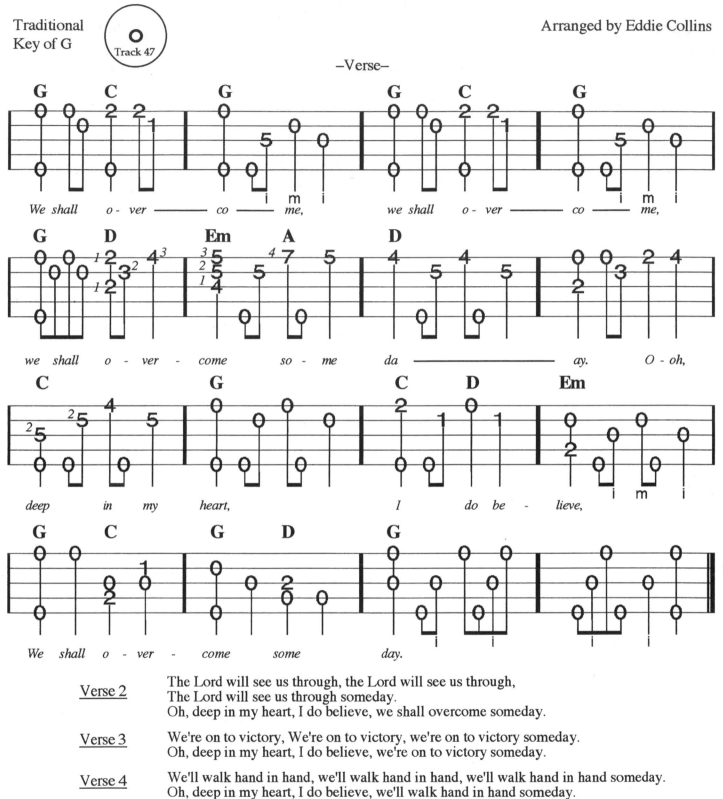

–Verse–

We shall o - ver —— co —— me, we shall o - ver —— co —— me,

we shall o - ver - come so - me da —————————— ay. O - oh,

deep in my heart, I do be - lieve,

We shall o - ver - come some day.

Verse 2   The Lord will see us through, the Lord will see us through,
The Lord will see us through someday.
Oh, deep in my heart, I do believe, we shall overcome someday.

Verse 3   We're on to victory, We're on to victory, we're on to victory someday.
Oh, deep in my heart, I do believe, we're on to victory someday.

Verse 4   We'll walk hand in hand, we'll walk hand in hand, we'll walk hand in hand someday.
Oh, deep in my heart, I do believe, we'll walk hand in hand someday.

Verse 5   We are not afraid, we are not afraid, we are not afraid today.
Oh, deep in my heart, I do believe, we are not afraid today.

Verse 6   The truth shall make us free, the truth shall make us free,
The truth shall make us free someday.
Oh, deep in my heart, I do believe, the truth shall make us free someday.

Verse 7   We shall live in peace, we shall live in peace, we shall live in peace someday.
Oh, deep in my heart, I do believe, we shall live in peace someday.

Where The Soul Of Man Never Dies

Traditional
Key of C

Arranged by Eddie Collins

Track 48

–Verse–

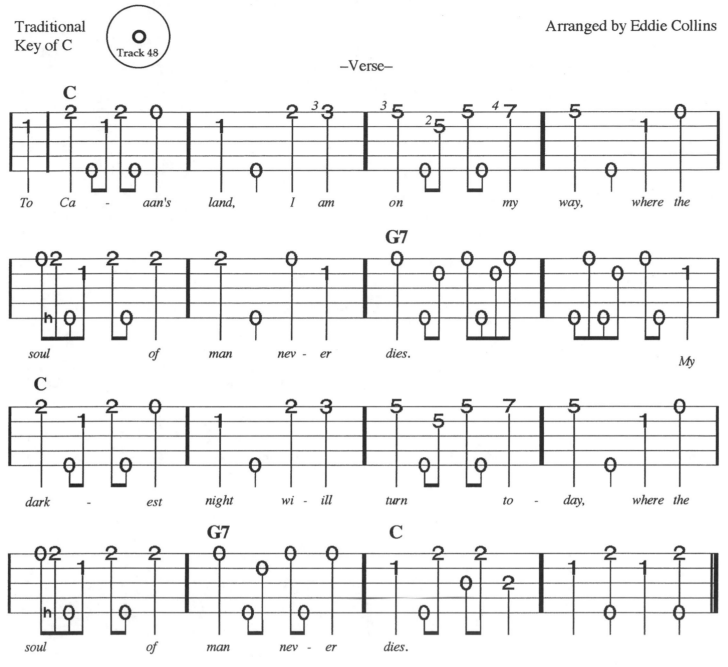

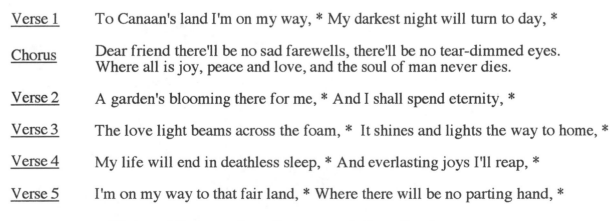

Verse 1	To Canaan's land I'm on my way, * My darkest night will turn to day, *
Chorus	Dear friend there'll be no sad farewells, there'll be no tear-dimmed eyes. Where all is joy, peace and love, and the soul of man never dies.
Verse 2	A garden's blooming there for me, * And I shall spend eternity, *
Verse 3	The love light beams across the foam, * It shines and lights the way to home, *
Verse 4	My life will end in deathless sleep, * And everlasting joys I'll reap, *
Verse 5	I'm on my way to that fair land, * Where there will be no parting hand, *

Note: All verses share the same melody as the chorus.

*Insert the lyric "Where the soul of man never dies." after each line of each verse.

THE STORY BEHIND GOSPEL GREATS FOR BANJO

I have written for numerous music magazines and specifically have been the "Beginner's Corner" columnist for *Banjo NewsLetter* for many years. The instruction in this book is based on three-finger style banjo patterned after the picking of Earl Scruggs. Part of the tradition of playing in this style is performing Gospel songs. As such, I have received numerous requests over the years to publish a collection of Gospel tunes performed in Scruggs style banjo.

When you hear the term "Gospel Banjo," many assume we are talking about tunes you hear at every bluegrass festival–tunes in the Southern Gospel tradition, such as "I'll Fly Away" and "I Saw The Light." While these definitely make for good banjo fare, I sought to cover new ground when compiling a book of Gospel tunes arranged for 5-string banjo. The following is a summary of my experiences as I pursued this project.

First off, I tried to familiarize myself with Gospel materials currently available to whet the appetite of banjo pickers. Most of what was available at the time of writing this was in the aforementioned Southern Gospel style. Thinking back to some of my childhood favorites, I realized that many famous hymns are far more suitable for organ using big, block chords, than for the rolling style of 5-string banjo. This doesn't mean the songs can't be performed on banjo, but that a different approach is needed. When reading from a traditional hymnal, most songs are presented in four-part choral arrangements for (lowest through highest) bass, baritone, alto and soprano. The highest note is usually the melody note. When trying to imitate the block chords of an organ, I chose to pinch two adjacent strings on the banjo. The top note of each pair is the melody supported by a harmony note. In this manner, you will clearly hear the melody without having to worry about it getting lost in a flurry of fill-in notes. "Jesus Loves Me" and "Joyful, Joyful We Adore Thee," among others, are performed in this style.

Lyrics have been placed below each melody note to give the learner the sense of where to stress notes in order to bring out the melody notes above the fill-notes of the rolls. Most of the songs in this collection have been transposed to the key of G, whereas a hymnal may have had them in Eb or F. There are a couple of tunes in C or D, but still no retuning from the standard key of G is ever needed throughout the book.

Of primary importance was to bring tunes to the banjo that I had never before heard performed on the instrument. Of the 40 songs included, it appears nearly 20 of them have not been previously arranged for banjo.

I consulted old hymnals, recordings and the Internet when researching the melodies to these songs and to insure they were in the public domain. There are no chords published in hymnals and organs often play additional "passing" chords that aren't needed, or appropriate, for banjo. I therefore would try to find additional recordings and/or other reproductions of the lyrics before settling on the best way to approach a particular song.

Lastly, I tried to create interesting arrangements that the vast majority of people learning to play banjo could grasp. As such, all the tunes are at an intermediate level with little melodic style picking required. The chord block style may be new to you, but is easy to follow. I hope you find the tunes both enjoyable and inspirational. Happy picking! Eddie Collins

More Great Books from Eddie Collins...

ASAP BLUEGRASS MANDOLIN
by Eddie Collins

This book/2-CD pack delivers the meat and potatoes of bluegrass mandolin way beyond just teaching fiddle tunes! Players will discover how to find their way around the neck using common double stops, develop creative back-up skills, play solos to vocal tunes in the style of Bill Monroe, make up their own solos, and a whole lot more. For the average learner, this pack represents nearly two years worth of lessons! Includes two (2) instructional CDs: one plays every example in the book, and the 2nd contains 32 songs performed by a bluegrass band with the mandolin parts separated on the right channel.

00001219...$24.95

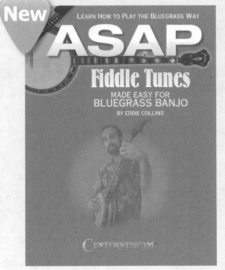

ASAP FIDDLE TUNES MADE EASY FOR BLUEGRASS BANJO
by Eddie Collins

This book/CD pack provides beginning and intermediate banjo players with two versions of 18 of the most popular fiddle tunes heard at bluegrass jam sessions. The "basic" solos generally begin on the first beat, contain lots of quarter notes, and use only simple rolls. The "intermediate" solos use more 8th notes and complex roles, and require more difficult formations of the left hand. Tunes include: Arkansas Traveler • Old Joe Clark • Red Wing • Salt Creek • Soldier's Joy • and more!
00001459...$19.99

P.O. Box 17878 - Anaheim Hills, CA 92817
(714) 779-9390   www.centerstream-usa.com

More Great Banjo Books from Centerstream...

BEGINNING CLAWHAMMER BANJO
by Ken Perlman

Ken Perlman is one of the most celebrated clawhammer banjo stylists performing today. In this new DVD, he teaches how to play this exciting style, with ample close-ups and clear explanations of techniques such as: hand positions, chords, tunings, brush-thumb, single-string strokes, hammer-ons, pull-offs and slides. Songs include: Boatsman • Cripple Creek • Pretty Polly. Includes a transcription booklet. 60 minutes.
00000330 DVD $19.95

INTERMEDIATE CLAWHAMMER BANJO
by Ken Perlman

Picking up where *Beginning Clawhammer Banjo* leaves off, this DVD begins with a review of brush thumbing and the single-string stroke, then moves into specialized techniques such as: drop- and double-thumbing, single-string brush thumb, chords in double "C" tuning, and more. Tunes include: Country Waltz • Green Willis • Little Billie Wilson • Magpie • The Meeting of the Waters • Old Joe Clark • and more! Includes a transcription booklet. 60 minutes.
00000331 DVD $19.95

CLAWHAMMER STYLE BANJO
A Complete Guide for Beginning and Advanced Banjo Players
by Ken Perlman

This handbook covers basic right & left-hand positions, simple chords, and fundamental clawhammer techniques: the brush, the "bumm-titty" strum, pull-offs, and slides. There is also instruction on more complicated picking, double thumbing, quick slides, fretted pull-offs, harmonics, improvisation, and more. Includes over 40 fun-to-play banjo tunes.
00000118 Book Only.. $19.95
00000334 DVD $39.95

THE EARLY MINSTREL BANJO
by Joe Weidlich

Featuring more than 65 classic songs, this interesting book teaches how to play the minstrel banjo like players who were part of various popular troupes in 1865. The book includes: a short history of the banjo, including the origins of the minstrel show; info on the construction of minstrel banjos, chapters on each of the seven major banjo methods published through the end of the Civil War; songs from each method in banjo tablature, many available for the first time; info on how to arrange songs for the minstrel banjo; a reference list of contemporary gut and nylon string gauges approximating historical banjo string tensions in common usage during the antebellum period (for those Civil War re-enactors who wish to achieve that old-time "minstrel banjo" sound); an extensive cross-reference list of minstrel banjo song titles found in the major antebellum banjo methods; and more. (266 pages)
00000325... $29.95

MELODIC CLAWHAMMER BANJO
A Comprehensive Guide to Modern Clawhammer Banjo
by Ken Perlman

Ken Perlman, today's foremost player of the style, brings you this comprehensive guide to the melodic clawhammer. Over 50 tunes in clear tablature. Learn to play authentic versions of Appalachian fiddle tunes, string band tunes, New England hornpipes, Irish jigs, Scottish reels, and more. Includes arrangements by many important contemporary players, and chapters on basic and advanced techniques. Also features over 70 musical illustrations, plus historical notes, and period photos.
00000412 Book/CD Pack $19.95

MINSTREL BANJO – BRIGGS' BANJO INSTRUCTOR
by Joseph Weidlich

The Banjo Instructor by Tom Briggs, published in 1855, was the first complete method for banjo. It contained "many choice plantation melodies," "a rare collection of quaint old dances," and the "elementary principles of music." This edition is a reprinting of the original Briggs' *Banjo Instructor*, made up-to-date with modern explanations, tablature, and performance notes. It teaches how to hold the banjo, movements, chords, slurs and more, and includes 68 banjo solo songs that Briggs presumably learned directly from slaves.
00000221... $12.95

MORE MINSTREL BANJO
by Joseph Weidlich

This is the second book in a 3-part series of intabulations of music for the minstrel (Civil War-era) banjo. Adapted from Frank Converse's *Banjo Instructor, Without a Master* (published in New York in 1865), this book contains a choice collection of banjo solos, jigs, songs, reels, walk arounds, and more, progressively arranged and plainly explained, enabling players to become proficient banjoists. Thorough measure-by-measure explanations are provided for each of the songs, all of which are part of the traditional minstrel repertoire.
00000258... $12.95

WITH MY BANJO ON MY KNEE
The Minstrel Songs of Stephen Foster
arr. for banjo by Daniel Partner
Historical notes by Edwin J. Sims

Here are some of the first and most popular songs ever written for banjo. Fascinating historical notes accompany this collection, describing the meaning of the songs, their place in history, the significance of the musicians who first performed them, and Foster himself, America's first professional songwriter. The complete original lyrics of each song and an extensive bibliography are included. The CD contains recordings of each arrangement performed on solo minstrel banjo.
00001179 Book/CD Pack $19.95

P.O. Box 17878 - Anaheim Hills, CA 92817
(714) 779-9390   www.centerstream-usa.com

Those using
Centerstream
Books & DVDs

The Competition